Job Interview

Self Help Guide To Win The Most Popular Job In The World

(The Best Answers And The Skills Needed To Get The Job Of Your Dreams And Have A Successful Life)

Joey Burdette

Published by Rob Miles

Joey Burdette

All Rights Reserved

Job Interview: Self Help Guide To Win The Most Popular Job In The World (The Best Answers And The Skills Needed To Get The Job Of Your Dreams And Have A Successful Life)

ISBN 978-1-989990-71-1

All rights reserved. No part of this guide may be reproduced in any form without permission in writing from the publisher except in the case of brief quotations embodied in critical articles or reviews.

LEGAL & DISCLAIMER

The information contained in this book is not designed to replace or take the place of any form of medicine or professional medical advice. The information in this book has been provided for educational and entertainment purposes only.

The information contained in this book has been compiled from sources deemed reliable, and it is accurate to the best of the Author's knowledge; however, the Author cannot guarantee its accuracy and validity and cannot be held liable for any errors or omissions. Changes are periodically made to this book. You must consult your doctor or get professional medical advice before using any of the suggested remedies, techniques, or information in this book.

Upon using the information contained in this book, you agree to hold harmless the Author from and against any damages, costs, and expenses, including any legal fees potentially resulting from the application of any of the information provided by this guide. This disclaimer applies to any damages or injury caused by the use and application, whether directly or indirectly, of any advice or information presented, whether for breach of contract, tort, negligence, personal injury, criminal intent, or under any other cause of action.

You agree to accept all risks of using the information presented inside this book. You need to consult a professional medical practitioner in order to ensure you are both able and healthy enough to participate in this program.

Table of Contents

INTRODUCTION 1

CHAPTER 1: HOW DO I PREPARE FOR THE JOB INTERVIEW? 4

CHAPTER 2: MAKING A PERSONAL ASSESSMENT OF YOURSELF TO GET READY 16

CHAPTER 3: ONLINE JOB SEARCHING BASICS 22

CHAPTER 4: SOFT SKILLS 40

CHAPTER 5: DEVELOP PROFESSIONAL EXPERTISE 55

CHAPTER 6: TARGETING THE OBJECTIVE 65

CHAPTER 7: FIRST INTERVIEW 70

CHAPTER 8: PERSPECTIVE 77

CHAPTER 9: TIPS FOR PREPARING FOR THE INTERVIEW .. 84

CHAPTER 10: WHY IS IT DIFFICULT TO LAND A JOB OF YOUR CHOICE? 95

CHAPTER 11: ONLY ONE FIRST IMPRESSION 98

CHAPTER 12: OVERALL PREPARATION 111

CHAPTER 13: HOW YOU CAN MAKE SURE THAT YOU ARE CHOSEN FOR AN INTERVIEW 118

CHAPTER 14: WHAT TO DO BEFORE THE INTERVIEW..... 128

CHAPTER 15: PRACTICE ASKING QUESTIONS 133

CHAPTER 16: PREPARING FOR THE INTERVIEW 138

- CHAPTER 17: YOUR QUESTIONS 144
- CHAPTER 18: INTERVIEW TECHNIQUES 149
- CHAPTER 19: INTERVIEW ETIQUETTE............................. 159
- CHAPTER 20: FILLING OUT AN APPLICATION 166
- CHAPTER 21: PROPER INTERVIEW SCHEDULING............ 169
- CHAPTER 22: THE INTERVIEW: FACING THE PANEL THE RIGHT WAY 176
- CONCLUSION... 179

Introduction

Job hunting can be one of the most stressful times in a person's life. Whether you are in-between jobs, looking to quit your present job or a fresh graduate, getting the job you want entails plenty of preparation both physically and mentally. If preparing or updating your resume and cover letter is not stressful enough, you still have to prep yourself for an interview.

In some ways, job hunting is like finding a date over the internet. You put up a profile online and sift through other people's profiles. You wait for matches and others to be interested. You get a match and you start connecting. You do not really know each other so you text, send messages or call sometimes. You look at pictures online, read through their Facebook walls and so on. Are you a good fit? Is he or she interesting enough for you? You do not actually meet until you know that you are really interested in each other. In addition, when that first actual date comes, you are nervous and want to make the great first impression.

A similar process goes on for job seeking. You look for jobs you are qualified for, research on companies, send your resume and wait for them to get back to you. You try to search some more and prepare for the possibility that they will like you and you also try to make sure your online presence will not jeopardize your career (so you Google yourself). Companies do not want to meet you if you have racy photos up (unless you want to work for porn or something). They will only want to see you if your qualifications fit. Finally, someone calls for an interview schedule. Moreover, when that interview comes, you are nervous and want to make the great first impression.

But here's the good news – if you are preparing for an interview, you can breathe a little bit easier known that at least you are qualified (or intriguing) enough to warrant an actual interview. To put it simply, you are at least one-step ahead of the job hunting pack. You have earned yourself a first date.

It's a good thing you got to grab this little reading material. It's all you'll ever need to get you prepared for (and get you through) a successful job interview. Read on and good luck!

Chapter 1: How Do I Prepare For The Job Interview?

"Go confidently in the direction of your dreams. Live the life you have imagined."——Henry David Thoreau

That's a very good question. How indeed do you prepare? See, the thing about job interviews is that they have a nasty tendency to quickly go downhill if you do not prepare in every single area. Your biggest fear should be not to forget what you were supposed to do and say, before, and while you're in the hot seat. You don't want your interview going up in smoke before your very eyes just because the employer doesn't exactly appreciate you deciding to do the planet a favor and skip your morning shower. He might not say it, but you'll probably just discover that the session ended a lot quicker than you expected without getting a chance to prove how suitable you are for the job. All that could happen because you woke up 20 minutes late and wouldn't have made it to the interview on time otherwise. There are lots of other things you should do to prepare before it's even time for the interview. Research your prospective employer as much as you possibly can. Every organization worth its salt has some kind of Internet presence, Take advantage of this and find out details of what your prospective employers do. It will impress your interviewer if you prove you have an extensive knowledge of the organization's products, services, customers, competitors, history and any recent news that might be of immediate relevance. Learn as much as you can about the duties and roles you might have to take in the case of you being employed and try to relate any previous experience or academic work you might have done to that role. The key to standing out in any interview is proving to the interviewer that you can add more value to the role you're being interviewed for than anyone of your competitors. You might be wondering how you can dig all that information up but the Internet and social media have made things really easy in that regard. Scour LinkedIn groups for key players with insider knowledge of workings of the company. Ask politely and you'll be surprised by how much of a response you'll get.

How do you pass that point across? Communicating effectively is the key. Remember, you will have a harder time trying to butter up the interviewer with slick sounding answers that have no conviction in them; you'd be better off just going with your gut. In other words, just be yourself.

The Purpose of Job Interviews

Job interviews are meant to find out how suitable you are for a particular job position and there are different ways employers achieve that purpose. Not every job interview is the same. You cannot expect every employer to interview you the same way that the previous one did, so obviously there is more than one way to tackle an interview.

Unfortunately, there are also more than one type of interview that you will have to learn how to come to terms with as well. You would probably have, or already have, come across the following types of interview sessions—

Employer Interviews— Employer interviews are designed by the internal HR of the organization to assess whether you fit the bill. In other words, they determine whether you are eligible for the job and the culture of the company in question. It is designed to take a look at your personality, ethics and skills and decide if they fit what the hiring company needs and is accustomed to. The interview is conducted by members of the relevant departments in person; the dynamics of the interview are often setup by HR.

The first level makes up the screening while the second level includes the candidates who made it through the initial screening stage. Land yourself invites to later interviews and you're just that bit closer to the big prize!

Recruitment Agency Interviews—Just as the name implies, these types of agencies are responsible for helping you find a job.

This also means that their main source of income is the employer (or recruiters) and not you as you might have thought.

Just because some agencies claim that they are there to help further your interests does not mean that they always end up doing so. In fact, most of these establishments are only designed to cater to the interests of the companies responsible for paying them.

In other words, they will try to put you in "any" job that can earn them their own living. This is why you need to look out for an agency that incorporates your needs as well as its own, at least to a reasonable extent. Land yourself an agency that does that and you can be sure that you will be trained in the tricks that will get you in any employer's good books.

Human Resources (HR) or Personnel Interviews—These types of interviews might seem to be the easy type since HR interviewers do not usually question you about any job related technical skill. This is because they are not the actual employers that you will need to answer to later.

It might also seem that these people might just want to "get to know you better" on a personal level but be careful, don't forget that these are trained professionals. In other words, they are "trained" to extract any info out of you. So it is better that you stay on your guard. Don't try to fool them on any issues either as they will most likely know that you are trying to do so.

Get that Paperwork Done

Besides the interview, your paper work will be all that will be working in your favor so make sure that it is in proper order. You need to make sure that you have all that will be of help to the employment process.

Your paperwork should (obviously) include your resume, copies of any certifications, degrees and every other document that pertains to the type of interview you are planning to undergo, initial job application, job description, as well as a copy of relevant application forms. Always have extra copies of everything in hand to give out as the need arises. Don't wait to start rushing to get any necessary printouts at the last minute. There are a few things I'd like to note about preparing your resume to attract the attention of a potential employer or recruiting agent. I cannot overstate the fact that the content and preparation of your resume is absolutely vital, after all, it's the major factor that will decide if you get called up for an interview or not.

Your resume should be designed to market the qualities you have towards meeting the needs of the specific employer that you are currently trying to get a job with. In simple words, it's more effective to prepare a separate resume for every individual job application. A new resume doesn't need to be done from scratch but it at least needs to be tailored to each specific employer. It might seem really tedious but it will certainly be worth it at the end. For example, in your job descriptions, try to tie specific tasks that you might have performed in a previous job to what you would be expected to do in a new role with your potential employer. If you do not have any previous work experience, maybe you're fresh out of college; list any assignments, research work or activity that you feel the employer might be interested in i.e. provided it is related to the job description.

The aim of the resume, like your overall objective, is to make you stand out from the hundreds of applications each employer is likely to receive, this however, should be written in as few words as possible, only get specific with the roles and tasks you've performed. You'll have ample opportunity to expand on your achievements later on In the course of the selection process.

Research the Organization

It pays to know your employer, and more so if you do your research. Make sure to research the type of company or organization that you are aiming to get in. This might also include where it is located and whether the location is feasible for you to get to if you do get hired.

If you want to go for larger corporations, you can make use of many written resources that can brief you about them as well as their preferences. These can be anything from business directories (that can be located in the reference section of local libraries) to public relations brochures the companies distribute themselves. However, nothing can beat the Internet as far as fast paced, in-depth research is concerned. This is also why almost every type of company and industry makes it a point to have extensive websites fully equipped to brief anyone about what they do. You might also want to do a good sweep of all the latest press releases and news from the company newsletter. Subscribe to any publications that each company might have if it is open to the public. Researching the management team as well as their responsibilities is always smart. You'd be surprised by how many candidates come to an interview without knowing what their prospective employer does. Social media would also be a huge asset in researching organizations. Twitter, Facebook and especially LinkedIn will provide an invaluable wealth of resources for your research efforts.

Know Yourself

Assessing your own strengths and weaknesses will help you out in the long run. It is crucial in the employment process. You should take the time to come to terms with your own strengths and weaknesses; then mold them in a way that caters to the employer's needs as well.

You can start off with your resume. Remember, employers or interviewers will be looking out for your strong points as well as weak points. So it is better that you ask yourself questions that will give you a clear understanding of where you stand at the moment. Questions like—

What are my major skills?

How have I chosen to utilize them where I worked before?

What are my major achievements and can I relate them to the employer's requirements as well?

What are my weaknesses?

The purpose of any job interview is to argue your case more effectively than the documents and credentials in your resume can. Just remember that you will only be able to do so if you have a thorough understanding of your strengths and weaknesses.

Also make it a point of asking plenty of relevant questions at interviews. This may help you keep track of where you might have gone wrong before and can also prevent you from making the same mistakes next time.

Be On Time!

I cannot stress this point enough! You do not want to end up giving a bad impression by coming late for an interview. Not only does this make a prospective employer think twice about hiring you, but it also makes you look unprofessional, incompetent, and unorganized. No one wants that vibe in their workplace and they'll go to any lengths to stop you from getting the job.

Try to get up at least 3 hours before you have to leave so that you can have plenty of time to calm those nerves and eat a healthy breakfast to sustain it. A word for the wise, try not to eat anything that's loaded with onions, garlic or anything else that could give you bad breath. Good first impressions remember? You don't want the only thing an interviewer remembers about the chat to be how badly your breath stinks, and how badly he/she had to try to keep from gagging. Believe me; if that happened, no one would want you anywhere near them every day, you might as well kiss that job good bye.

Chapter 2: Making A Personal Assessment Of Yourself To Get Ready

When most people are preparing for a job interview one of the first things they begin to wonder is "what will I wear to my job interview?" You may think that wearing your most expensive suit or outfit is the way to go when choosing clothing for an interview, but it is not always the best choice. If you are trying to look like you are the right one for a particular position, then there are a few critical things that you need to get right during the preparation of your job interview.

It is important that you match your outfit deems appropriate for the job that you are applying for. This will help the interviewer to view you as the right person for the job. Make sure that your dressing is proper for the interview—suit and tie for example. An easy way to assess this situation is to ask yourself these simple questions:

Are you really serious about finding a new job?

Are you ready to make that change in career that you have wanted, but have kept putting it off for one reason or another?

Do you want to make certain that you are giving your future boss the impression that you are the most suitable candidate for the position you are applying for?

Do you pay attention to your personal hygiene and grooming like neat and tidy hair in addition to your dress?

If you are truly serious about making a good impression in your upcoming interview, and seriously want to get this job, you should have answered yes to all of the above questions.

Giving a positive answer to these questions shows that you have the proper personality that will more than likely dress well for a job interview. Below are three basic suggestions to help you get started on preparing for a job interview.

1. Having a Desire to Dress Properly in order to Impress your Future Boss

The way that you dress for an interview is going to play a very critical role in your job interview. You do not want to take your appearance for a job interview lightly, and just focus on preparing for the interview questions and answers as this could be your downfall. You could fail in your interview the moment your boss sets eyes upon you and gets the impression that you are careless and sloppy. They are not going to want to hire someone that they view as not taking the interview seriously, they have doubts whether you will focus and pay attention to details that are important in your job.

Take for example that the future boss has two candidates to choose from, if one looks sloppy and tired that is the one that they are going to eliminate. You do not want to enter an interview looking like you just rolled out of bed.

When you are at the point where you have a deep desire to impress your future boss and give your best during an interview, that is when you are well on your way to getting your dream job!

You must remember that dressing up for your interview is much more than just looking good, or giving a good first impression to your interviewer. This is part of the critical strategy that is going to lead you into landing that dream job that you deserve.

2. Thinking about What to Wear for Your Job Interview

Do not dress base on your fashion taste, instead dress suitable for the job description that you are applying for. Do your research on this particular job, as well as the company business overall, this will help you to easily decide what to wear for the interview.

If this particular job you are applying for involves meeting business clients, you should wear a business suit to the interview. If on the other hand you are going to apply for a job that is going to involve wearing more casual outfits then go with business casual.

Just remember when going to an interview never put on jeans no matter how casual dress the job itself is.

3. Understanding Requirements of the Job
Do some research on the company, learn and understand as much as you can about the job itself. Learning exactly what is in the job description so you know what is going to be required of you in this position. Prepare yourself by visiting the company website to know more. One of the most common questions a future employee will ask is "how much do you know about us?" Or they may ask "why do you choose them or want to be employed at their company?"

If you are unable to answer questions about their business and show them that you completely understand the responsibility of your job, they may think that you are a money chaser who is just after the job for the money.

Pay attention to their press releases as well as business case studies. You can find valuable information that will tell you what the company is best at, and what's their next move going to be. You can mix this information into your interview to show your boss that you are serious about getting this job and are excited about the possible prospect of working for their company.

You can also use this information that you gathered to ask your future boss questions. Often, they will ask whether you have any questions for them. Take this opportunity to inform him that you did some research on the company. Make sure the question that you ask is related to the company. Perhaps you could mention for example that you liked that they are using a wireless connection service. The interviewers will get excited that you have questions related to the company, and they will enjoy giving you the details on how changes within the company came about.

This becomes more like a business meeting when you are talking about the running of the company and different elements of it. You will make your future boss feels that you are a good fit for the job.

Chapter 3: Online Job Searching Basics

Applying to Advertised Openings

In this section, you'll learn valuable, easy steps to significantly increase the number of calls for interviews you receive as you apply to advertised openings.

Follow the job application instructions carefully. I repeat, follow the application instructions to a T. You would be surprised that many people don't do this.

Identify the Important Decision Makers

You know how your heart jumps when you receive a neatly prepared envelope displaying your name spelled correctly...and how your heart sinks when you get sent a letter with "Resident" on the label, or your name misspelled? Hiring managers and resume screeners experience the same excitement and disappointment as they sort through the many applications they receive. So it's worth it to invest some time and effort in finding and correctly spelling the resume screeners' names. Sure, you can always default to the standard (and pretty boring) "Dear Sir or Madam," but I recommend that you use one or more of these methods:

• Use a search engine to research contact names. In many cases you can locate the names of department managers and hiring coordinators within companies by simply entering the correct keywords into a search engine, such as Google. For instance, you could enter, "Vice President Marketing Great Balls of Fire, Inc." to see if his or her name is listed anywhere on the Internet. Or try, "Human Resources Great Balls of Fire, Inc." to locate a representative within the personnel department. As you uncover names using this method, be sure to verify that the contacts are still currently in those positions by executing this next step...

• Call the company directly and ask for the names of the key contacts. Simply phone the business and say, "I would like to verify the name and spelling of the head of the widgets department." If you have a name that you've researched on the Internet, you can also say, "Is it still Jane Williams?"

• If you're asked, "Why do you need this information?" answer with, "I'm responding to your job ad and I want to make sure I spell her name correctly." If this step makes you nervous, enlist the help of a friend or job search supporter to do it for you. And if the ad clearly states, "No calls," don't call!

"Yikes, call the company directly! Won't they get mad?" I know, I know...the thought of calling a potential employer directly to gather info about contacts can seem pretty scary. Many job seekers fear that the hiring manager might actually pick up the phone (she might), and that for some reason she won't like the sound of your voice. Other job seekers worry that a mean receptionist will tell them to go jump in a lake. So yes, it can seem scary to call. Yet consider this: The person at the company who answers the phone ends up giving us the information we want 75 percent of the time. Those are pretty good odds! And if they don't give us the name, they don't yell at us. Instead, they say something like, "I'm not allowed to give out that information." Some adverts will ask you not to phone the company. If this is what they say, well then don't phone the company. I know I certainly don't want 1000's of applicants calling me. Emailing me is fine, but not calling.

Mention Any Mutual Acquaintances

Staying on the topic of names, you could mention any mutual acquaintances in your cover letter. For example, let's say that Lance Mercer, a vendor you know from Spiffy Products, told you about an opening at Great Balls of Fire, Inc., and encouraged you to apply. He knows the VP of Marketing at Great Balls of Fire, Inc., personally.

In the first paragraph of your cover letter, you could write this:

Lance Mercer, a mutual acquaintance, told me about the opening within your company and encouraged me to apply.

Mentioning Lance's name will give you instant credibility, and again, will help you stand out from the other applicants. If you don't have a mutual acquaintance, consider sending a message to people m your network to see whether anyone has a connection to the hiring manager or human resources representative. Again, here you are making an effort.

Research the Company's Priorities

Similar to including keywords from a job description in your materials, it's also a good idea to incorporate phrases that relate to the company's priorities. Spend a few minutes researching the hiring company on the Internet. Be on the lookout for key phrases that describe the company's mission, culture, and products. This is not applicable for all job applicants and in some instances, might be more important at the job interview itself. Then find ways to work that verbiage into your materials. For instance, you could write something like this:

Your company's focus on creating and maintaining sustainable operations is admirable, and is in line with my own values. When I worked at Company X, I organized and launched the first sustainability review task force...

Create a Flawless Application

When you apply to an advertised opening, some businesses will require you to complete a formal application, by filling out either an online or hardcopy document. To improve your chances of being selected for an interview, follow these formal application guidelines:

• Complete the application in full. To you, some of the questions asked on an application might seem silly, redundant, or prying. However, if a company uses an application in its hiring process, you need to take it seriously, and complete it fully and without errors. This is a really important part to take note of.

• Don't omit information about pay. Instead, include a range when providing information about former salary (list starting and ending—and factor in bonuses and benefits), and write "open" or "negotiable" when responding to questions about desired compensation. But still give a figure.

Worried about including salary information when a company asks for it? You're right...it can feel like an employer is invading your privacy by asking something so personal. "What right do they have to ask?" you might wonder. Keep in mind that for larger employers especially, their goal is to standardize and streamline their hiring processes to deal with the thousands of job applications they receive each year. Gathering information about your pay is one way those companies can streamline their sorting processes to determine whether you're a fit for a position that interests you. For this reason, it's important to include this when you're asked for this information on an application or a low-high range detailing the upper and lower ends of your former compensation. Even though it might make you squirm a little, don't leave these blocks on an application blank—otherwise, you could be booted from consideration. If an applicant replies and says, —"Will discuss in interview," I think, sorry, you've refused even to give us the upper and lower ends of your salary requirements, you are not making the interview. This might sound harsh, but interviews take up a huge amounts of time and if an applicant does not want to give us any details of their required salary, we don't want to waste everyone's time.

Send Applications to Both the Hiring Manager and the HR Rep

This is an easy-to-execute activity that generates great results. As you prepare an application in response to a job opening, plan to submit materials to both the hiring manager (the person you would end up reporting to) as well as to the human resources representative. Most job hunters send their materials only to human resources. Yet keep in mind the HR reps are not the ultimate decision makers —that power lies with your future boss! So send her a package, too. Again, this depends on whether you are applying to a job advertisement, or just merely applying to a company you want to work for that has no job advertisements.

Keep Records of What You've Submitted

Down the line, when the hiring company calls to schedule an interview, you might need to refer to the materials you submitted. For this reason, it's a good idea to print and file a copy of each of your applications, cover letters, and resumes.

The vast majority of job searchers put very little time into customizing their resumes and cover letters. By putting in just a little extra effort on each application—researching appropriate contact names, finding out and including a sentence or two about the company, sending a set of materials to both the HR rep and the hiring manager—you can quickly and easily rise above the crowd of other applicants, and greatly increase your chances of being called in for an interview. A few extra minutes invested when you prepare your applications can shorten your job search and open doors to many more attractive job opportunities!

When it comes to preparing job applications, the easiest route is to slap a "Dear Sir or Madam" on your cover letter and submit it along with your standard resume. For job seekers, this can seem "safe" as well as easy. Yet this approach doesn't usually generate very good results. By investing a little more effort—and taking steps that might make your heart pound, such as calling the potential employer to obtain the hiring manager's name—you can quickly set yourself apart from the competition and greatly improve your job search results. Will it make you squirm a little? Probably. But this is an ideal time to build your courage muscles!

Address the application directly to the person who has placed the advertisement. Often this person's name is given, if not, find out who to address your application to.

Approaching Companies without Job Postings

There is a "hidden job market" — that mysterious pool of openings that aren't obvious to the typical job searcher. In this section, you're going to find out how to dip into that resource and significantly expand the number of job opportunities available to you. Making use of this single job hunting method can quickly transform your job search from so-so to Go, Go! So read on to find out how to put this exciting, powerful job search tool to work for you.

If you want to work for a company that has not posted a job advertisement, go for it and send your application. Then follow up, follow up and follow up. Tell them what you can do for them, how you can contribute and be an asset to their business. All business owners want someone who has a great attitude, works hard and is an asset to their business.

So, from my perspective as a business owner, if we received job applications and have not posted an ad, I am usually delighted. We are a growing business and often need more staff. The whole process of posting job ads, going through the applications, interviews etc. is tiring and time consuming.

So if we receive a job application out of the blue, I take it seriously and always hope that this person we can employ. Often they are not suitable, for example, recently a competitor retrenched staff and one of their retrenched staff applied to work for us. In her email she implied that she would bring their client list with her. This is not ethical and not the right way to do business and we have not employed her. Integrity is at all times important to us and I want to hire people with good ethics. If a candidate approaches us and might be suitable and looks like a great candidate, I will do my best to find a place in our business for her or him. Many businesses will create a position for a good candidate. Remember that. Dream big, work hard and above all, take action. Apply for the job you want.

You know you have great skills, experience, and talents to offer to an employer. But do employers know about you? Chances are, they don't. In fact, it's very likely that the majority of companies who would want to hire you don't even know you exist. However, you can easily turn this situation around by following the steps described below.

Create Your Target List

These are employers who can potentially benefit from what you have to offer.

Prepare Powerful Letters of Introduction, but keep them short!

• Name and address information: This information will be customized to include specifics pertaining to a target employer on your list.

• Opening paragraph: Instead of referring to an advertised job, as you would if there were an actual opening available, you are instead introducing yourself as a potential resource.

• Bullet statements: Instead of listing a specific requirement (again, because you aren't responding to a job ad), you'll need to keep your bullet statements more generic.

Are you just now realizing that I'm suggesting that you mail your resume and letter of introduction to employers who aren't even advertising for employees? And does the idea of this make you uncomfortable? Well, you're not alone in this concern. Most job searchers worry about things like, "What if the employer isn't even interested? What if she's perfectly happy with the employees she has now? What if she thinks I'm an idiot for mailing her my resume? What if she immediately dumps my materials in the trash?" Yes, there are a lot of "what-ifs" and unknowns when it comes to approaching companies directly. Yet consider this: Many employers would be thrilled to consider you as a resource, if they only knew you were available! Sure, you'll experience some rejection with this activity. But you also experience rejection when you apply to advertised positions—so what's the difference? Even more important to consider is the fact that many employers are in desperate need of someone with your experience and talents. So read on, and chances are you'll feel more comfortable with this idea as you learn more about it.

Confidentiality in your cover letter.

An Example

Imagine that you are a successful business owner. You run Coolio Company, and your work is meaningful and interesting. For the most part, you love what you do. The only little fly in the ointment is that occasionally, you end up with a member on your team who isn't working out.

In fact, you have that problem right now. Three months ago you hired a new office manager, Lena, to replace Jill, who had been your office manager for two years. Jill had been great in her job, but she moved out of state, so you went through a hiring process to replace her.

The hiring process was a bit of a nightmare. You advertised on www.monster.com and ran an ad in the local paper, and were flooded with applications — more than 10000! You spent hours going through those resumes, but in the end, only eight applicants really looked as if they'd fit the job. You called in five of them for interviews, hoping to find a new "Jill" among the bunch.

It didn't work out that way. Of the five candidates you interviewed, only two seemed acceptable, but neither of them really impressed you. Still, Jill had already been gone for two weeks, and you were in desperate need of an office manager, so you offered the job to Lena.

That was three months ago. Since then, it has become more and more obvious that Lena isn't working out, and you've started to think about firing her. But the idea of running another ad, interviewing people again, and still not knowing whether you'll find someone better has held you back.

Just then, the daily mail arrives. Flipping through the stack, you notice an envelope hand-addressed to you. You pull it out and open it. It's a letter and resume from Charlotte, and she's writing to introduce herself as a potential office manager for Cool-o Company "Hmmm," you think. "Could this be the answer I've been looking for?" You carefully read through her resume and are impressed with what she has to offer. But just then Lena sticks her head into your office. "You have a call from one of our important customers." Distracted, you set Charlotte's letter in a stack of papers and forget about it for a while.

A few days later, you arrive at your office and check your voice mail. There's a message from Charlotte! She says, "I'm following up on a resume I sent you a few days ago. I'd like to set a time to meet you briefly. Would Thursday morning or Friday afternoon this week work for you? My phone number is...."

Wow, this Charlotte chick really seems to have her act together! You phone her to set up a meeting. What could it hurt? She might be just what you're looking for—without the hassle of needing to go through another complicated hiring process.

Decision makers —especially wise, growth-oriented ones (the kinds you want to work for) are always on the lookout for quality talent. So if you, like Charlotte, were to present yourself directly to some of those decision makers, you would very likely discover that those managers and business owners would be open to talking with you. Yet, get this: Less than 10 percent of job searchers ever go to the effort of approaching potential employers directly.

As a result, multitudes of job opportunities exist in the world of work, but job searchers aren't going after them!

So, yes, yes, yes, approaching companies directly is worth it! Just try a few and see. I predict that you'll be very pleased with the results.

I know that the idea of approaching companies directly is one of the most frightening for job seekers to try. But just like other intimidating things you've attempted in your life—riding a two-wheeler bike, or asking someone out on a date, for instance—trying new things (although scary) can take you to new, wonderful places you've only dreamed of.

And the most important thing is to go for it, follow up, offer to work for less initially and tell the company that you really want to work for them. Know why if they ask you!

Chapter 4: Soft Skills

A while back, one of the survey questions on Family Feud was to **name something you know is real, even though you can't see it.** Psyched up, the faster button pusher shouted, "bigfoot." To which, Steve Harvey and the audience erupt in laughter. Like the survey question, soft skills are one of those things employers know exist, even though they can't immediately be seen. Peter Schutz, former President and C.E.O. of Porsche used to say, "Hire character. Train Skill."

So how do interviewees showcase something that isn't easy to convey through traditional methods? And what are the soft skills employers most want?

There are two ways to showcase your soft skills. The smart interviewee will find a way to incorporate both into the selection process.

On Paper. As mentioned above, the first is to include a few soft skills on your resume. You might feel a bit weird about claiming non-concrete attributes. After all, how do you prove them? Isn't labeling your soft skills like bragging? Possibly, but remember this is your chance to sell yourself. If you don't have the confidence to sing your own praises, who will? Besides, employers are more than aware of the importance of these skills. Warren Buffet once mused, "Somebody once said that in looking for people to hire, you look for three qualities: integrity, intelligence, and energy. And if you don't have the first, the other two will kill you."

A word to the wise. While soft skills are easier to fake than hard skills, most employers have plenty of experience spotting fakers. After all they often spend days interviewing candidates for the position you hope to land. So don't fake it and don't add soft skills you haven't mastered.

A good rule of thumb is to use a one to two model. Add one soft skill for every two hard skills on your resume. But be sincere in the soft skills you highlight. Only capitalize on those standout skills or traits you feel are your best.

Bring those soft skills home during the interview process. Prepare anecdotes or have a few situational stories ready to share in which you clearly displayed the soft skills you want to convey to a potential employer. For example, if you want to showcase reliability, relate an event in which your reliability helped save the day or benefitted a former family member, team, or boss.

During the Interview. In some situations, you can demonstrate the soft skills you wish to highlight during the interview process. Good listening skills, creativity, and problem solving are all skills that can be seen and proven in real time.

John Sesay, co-author of **A Lion Has No Horns** builds his book around the tactics he used to save an interview through a combination of soft and hard skills. During the interview, he noticed how distracted his interviewer was. She was so distracted, that he began to wonder if she was taking the interview seriously, or if he was just there to fulfil an EEO requirement.

He noticed that she got most distracted when people dropped reports into the basket on her shelf. She kept reaching up to touch the shelf every time they came by. At first, he thought, she was distracted by the constant flow of workers, but they were quiet and respectful as they soundlessly dropped their work off. The more he watched he realized that the woman's shelf was slightly askew. He finally worked up the courage to ask her if there was a problem with her shelf. She told him that, it had been a problem for over a week and that despite putting in multiple requests for maintenance to fix it, it had yet to be done.

Sesay asked if he might take a closer look at the shelf, which she allowed. Then told her he could fix it, if she could find him a few simple tools. Within minutes, he displayed strong observation, problem solving, and leadership skills, as well as a good dose of empathy. Of course he had the hard skills to carry through and fix the shelf. All of which helped him in the end.

While not everyone will be lucky enough to be presented with a situation like Sesay during an interview, there usually are ample opportunities to showcase soft skills. So, what are the top soft skills employers seek?

According to a 2019 LinkedIn Survey, the top five soft skills employers are looking for are:

Creativity

Persuasion

Collaboration

Adaptability

Time management

I would argue an additional five skills:

Reliability

Energy

Honesty

Eagerness to learn

Empathy

…also rank high on many employers' must have lists. Let's look at each of them and why they rank among the most important traits employers seek.

Creativity is the foundation on which everything else is built. Whether you're a graphic artist, teacher, or engineer, creativity innovates and problem solves. It brings something new, unique, and different to the table. It helps companies to work smarter not harder. Creative people have great imaginations and aren't afraid to ask "what if?" It's not difficult to see why employers look for creative souls.

Potential employees can showcase their creativity in a number of ways from the design style of their resumes, to providing a link to a website that showcases a project they've helped create, to how they answer interview questions. The possibilities are endless.

Jeff Bezos, founder of Amazon believes creativity and innovation are one and the same. He's quoted as saying, "One of the only ways to get out of a tight box is to invent your way out."

Persuasion is a must for any sales position, but it's also helpful for many other careers. Those with the power of persuasion hold great power. Whether it's fundraising, convincing a board to adopt a new curriculum, or lobbying for new laws, those that can easily and diplomatically sway others to a desired opinion are great assets to any company.

Collaboration or fitting easily into a team is definitely a welcome asset in most industries. Steve Jobs, co-founder of Apple built his business model on collaboration. "My model for business is The Beatles: They were four guys that kept each others' negative tendencies in check; they balanced each other. And the total was greater than the sum of the parts."

While collaboration might seem obvious, the reality is many organizations face personality conflicts. Big egos, the need for power, competition, past histories and more can lead to fractures within organizations. Sometimes these situations brew for years, creating toxic work environments.

Those who are willing to work together, rift off each other, credit the team for good work, and so on make for a more desirable work environment and therefore are more desirable employees. Some qualities collaborators exhibit include: conflict management, strong listening skills, giving positive feedback, and the ability to mediate and negotiate.

Adaptability fits well with the old adage the "best-laid plans…" It's an old Scottish saying that basically means planning for something doesn't guarantee its success. That couldn't be truer in the workplace. Whether it's a key piece of equipment that breaks at the worst moment, an employee who doesn't show up, or a shipment that doesn't arrive, there will always be reasons for flexibility and back-up plans. Those who can go with the flow or hop into a different position without complaint when needed most rank high on employers must have lists. Those who are adaptable remain calm in a crisis, are able to analyze a situation and quickly self-manage or perhaps even organize a small group to problem solve or cover a needed task.

Time Management is akin to money. Those who can work smarter not harder usually accomplish tasks in less time, which saves money. In the book **The 4-Hour Work Week,** author Timothy Ferriss introduces the concept that time is just as valuable as money. The more of it that we can save, the more we can devote to the tasks we really want to be doing. Likewise, the more a company can save, the more it can devote to doing what it was intended to do as opposed to the mechanics or housekeeping of the business. Time managers are self-starters, that not only know how to plan, but also delegate.

Reliability doesn't take much to accomplish. After all it's about showing up, being dependable, and following through. Yet it's a critical soft skill for potential hires. Could you imagine what would happen if you planned a transcontinental trip and the pilot didn't show up? You don't necessarily have any desire to become friends with the pilot or even know her name, but you absolutely need her to show up for her job. And you expect that when she arrives, she not only knows how to properly fly the plan, but can do it well enough to get you safely to your destination.

In the same way, an employer may not want to be your best friend, but they count on those they hire to do a specific job well and in the allotted amount of time. If you want to display reliability during the interview process first and foremost arrive on time. Then make sure to share a past experience in which your reliability was key.

Energy is often equated with positivity. Those who have tins of energy can sweep in and brighten the disposition of an entire organization. Someone with energy is motivated to go the extra mile, work quickly and competently. Likewise, those who lack energy are often seen as weights pulling everyone down with them. They distract others from their work or cause others to pick up their slack. It's not difficult to see why employers enjoy hiring those with lots of energy. They just seem to make life easier.

Honesty is a soft skill that was somewhat overlooked in the past, but is enjoying a resurgence in the professional world. Sometimes also referred to as ethics, social responsibility, or integrity, this soft skill has made a huge comeback especially in environmental, eco-friendly, grassroots type businesses. But it has also made it to the corporate world—where cutting corners to save a dime is seen as less and less desirable.

Honesty isn't just about doing what looks right to the outside world, it's about expressing values on which an organization was founded. Most organizations today have a mission statement or history on their websites. Find out what's important to the founding members. If their values fit with yours, use similar language during your interview to convey your honesty.

Eagerness to Learn might seem a bit counterintuitive but nothing could be further from the truth. Most employers understand there will be a learning curve when a new employee joins their organization. Think of it like learning to drive a car. They expect you to know how to drive, but understand that you may only know how to drive an automatic while they operate a manual. Or better yet, maybe you know how to drive both, but it's still wise to have a look around the new car and learn where everything is before putting it into gear and taking off. It's great to display your knowledge and know-how, but it equally important to listen and learn. Those who do come to understand not only what is expected of them, but what the organization wants to do, where it hopes to go, and how those within it relate to each other.

Empathy is the ability to understand another person's situation and relate to it. In business it's the exact opposite of "don't let the door hit you on the way out." Businesses and organizations that care about their customers and employees generally last longer and don't have to work quite as hard. Think about it, empathy inspires loyalty. When an organization is empathetic, it retains those who continue to fund it, which is much easier than constantly finding new clients and customers. Those who are empathic consider the needs of others and generally display interpersonal communication skills.

Smile. Some simple ways to display empathy include smiling, calling people by name, remembering them or learning something about them before hand to mention during an interview and taking time to listen.

Arte Nathan, who was the Chief Human Resources Officer for several Vegas Casinos, used to say, "You can't teach employees to smile. They have to smile before you hire them."

Make A Wish. One of the most powerful tools of empathy is the wish. A wish is a way to give someone something without necessarily really doing it. It needs to be sincere, but an example would be if an angry customer came in demanding something be fixed. An empathic employee might start by smiling, and calling the customer by name. Then listening without interrupting. They might then ask the customer what they would like to be done about the situation. Even if it something that the employee can't fix, they could say something like, "I can see how upsetting this is to you. I wish I could fix it for you right now. Let me see if I can find someone who can better help you." Often just the ability to listen, display empathy, and give the customer what they need in the form of a wish, goes a long way to fixing a problem and retaining that customer of the future. In an interview situation, you might share an empathetic experience or suggest a way the organization could display more empathy.

Placement of Soft Skills

Now that you understand soft skills and hopefully have identified a few of your own it's time to put them on your resume. Place the "Skills" section directly below your name and contact information in three columns across the top. Then list 9 to 12 bulleted skills that highlight your abilities. That gives employers a better idea of who you are and what you can do for their organization than any goal statement.

Chapter 5: Develop Professional Expertise

All jobs require workers to continue strengthening and learning skills which can help them perform their tasks efficiently and effectively. With continuous professional development, they can be assured of promotion or empowerment to lead other people in the company. A person, who wants to develop professional expertise, must find ways to grow his skills and knowledge so he can be a recognized expert within his company or even industry.

You must make it your goal to become a life-long learner. You have to develop your professional expertise in order to be updated with current trends and information, which are relevant to your field. It is best that you continue your education by obtaining a graduate or even a post-graduate diploma. You can also get a special certification.

You can read journals, books, and articles related to your field of experience. These source materials can offer information which can be important as you continue to develop yourself professionally. In addition, you can follow social media accounts and blogs. You can connect with other professionals in your field so that you can learn form them. You can also attend conferences so that you can network with other people in your field. You can also participate in thought-provoking workshops and discussions.

If you want to develop professional expertise, you can also seek mentors, who can guide and teach you. Older leaders or employees from your office can be your mentors. You can also attend seminars or listen to podcasts of experts in your industry. You can learn from the biographies of people who made a great contribution in your field.

You can also join a professional group. You can meet with other professionals in your industry to hone your skills. You can form a discussion group in your office and talk about experiences and problems that you've all encountered recently. You can even have a professional blog where you can write about your experiences in your work. You can publish articles in professional journals. You can clarify your thoughts by writing about them. Lastly, you have to find opportunities to further build your skills.

How Professional Skills Can Be Built

Evaluate Your Skills

You have to know your strengths so that you can use them in your quest for better careers. It is important that you understand your strengths as you create your resume, take on leadership roles, explore career possibilities, and get yourself interviewed for jobs. If you understand your strengths, you'll know what skills you have to improve on. When you assess your strengths, you can list the top 3 areas you need to improve. For example, you realized you have to enhance your planning and coordinating skills, teamwork skills, and public speaking skills. Then, you can check the job description of the work you're applying for to see if you meet the requirements.

Set Goals To Enhance Professional Skills

After listing the top 3 areas you need to enhance, you have to set specific goals for each area. Your goals must be Specific, Measurable, Achievable, Realistic, and Timely. For instance, if you want to speak in public well, your SMART goals may be: To deliver 4 training presentations during organizational meetings by the end of the year.

Develop An Action Plan

In creating an action plan, you can use the SMART goals you set. In the example above, possible action steps can be:

1. Determine important information and topics to train the group members by January 31, 2015.

2. Draft and practice the presentations made from the topics identified in (1) by February 28, 2015.

3. Train the group members in the quarterly meetings beginning in March, 2015.

Look For Opportunities To Practice The Professional Skills

After creating the action plan, you then have to prepare to make the presentations to your group members. If you belong to an association of professionals, you can volunteer to deliver training presentations to them on certain topics.

Professional Skills You Need To Master

Communication Skills

For you to succeed in your career, you must learn to communicate with clarity and confidence. Your words must be powerful and you must effectively deliver what you have to say. You won't be hired or promoted if you don't communicate your ideas clearly and engagingly.

Relationship Building

You can't be a loner if you want to be hired or be promoted. You have to work well with your managers, peers, and colleagues. You have to develop supportive relationships in your workplace so you can succeed.

Decision-making

Decisions have to be made everyday. It is important that you know how to make them so that they are aligned with what you want. These decisions must also create new opportunities and add to your experience and skill base. Business decisions must be able to create the most desired results for the company. A lot of people don't know how to assess with discernment. They don't know how make cost-benefit analysis to make the best decision.

Leadership

There is really no well-crafted training guide on becoming an inspiring manager and leader. True leaders must be able to demonstrate leadership traits, actions, and behaviors which differentiate them from the rest of the pack. Therefore, it is important for you to know how to motivate, inspire, and empower others as you strive for your own success.

Negotiating and Advocating Your Causes and Yourself

In your career, you have to continuously negotiate and advocate for everything that you are concerned about. You have to learn to speak up and support your own causes.

Career Management and Planning

You have to learn to manage your career proactively so that it grows in the right direction. You have to know what contributions you want to make in your industry. You can't just float around aimlessly and miss those opportunities.

Finding Work-Life Balance

You'll surely struggle as you seek to balance life and work. You must understand how to prioritize things that really matter to you. You have to negotiate the conflicting demands of your home and career.

Enforcing Boundaries

As invisible barriers, boundaries control the flow of input and information within and outside the system. If you don't understand yourself and fail to make a protective and appropriate boundary around you, you'll find it difficult to succeed professionally. You have to develop and enforce such boundaries daily. You must learn to manage your decision making, your emotions, your career planning, your communications and yourself in order to shape your professional life.

Some Interview Questions And Answers

Question: What is your professional development plan for the next year?

Why this may be asked: The interview wants to know if you're aware of your weaknesses and if you're abreast with the current trends in the industry.

Possible answers: First, you have to ensure that you have a professional development plan because you don't know if you have to move to another job in the near future.

If you're a project manager, you can say, "I am strengthening my business intelligence skills. I have taken advanced ERP applications seminar."

If you're a hospital administrator, you can say, "I read a lot of articles about electronic health systems to help create clinical quality measures. I have taken a seminar about it."

If you're applying for a job which requires presentation skills, you can say, "I have to improve on my presentation skills by enrolling in a workshop on how to optimize presentation tools like PowerPoint. I got a lot of positive feedback from my seminar attendees about my presentations but I still have to enhance my skills."

Question: What's a time you exercised leadership?

Why this may be asked: The interviewer is interested with your story. He has to know what you did in the past.

Possible answer: Your story must be memorable and believable. It must be able to show how your overall leadership became part of an important experience. For you share the right stories, you have to know the job description in order to highlight the featured soft skills. You have to search for words like "comfortable with multitasking", "ability to work independently and with a team", or "strong communication skills". Then, you have to create a story about how you showed these skills in your experience.

Your story must be effective. You can make a statement prior to your story. You can say, "I learned early on that it is ok to disagree with a superior if I have data to prove my hunches." This way, the interviewer will know that you use your past experience for future disagreements.

Lastly, you have to end your story in a strong manner. You can connect it to the position you're applying for. You can explain quickly how your experiences can be beneficial in the position.

Chapter 6: Targeting The Objective

Targeting Individual Firms

Now that you have identified your objectives, established SMART goals, and have gotten into the right frame of mind, it's time to get down to business. At this stage of the game, your goal is to identify the firms that comprise your target industry. If you are new to the industry, researching the various firms that comprise it is a good way to become familiar with the landscape. At the very least, you will want to have a basic understanding of the industry and how it works. The same rule applies for aspiring entrepreneurs seeking advice from established entrepreneurs as it does for those seeking to find employment with organizations. Not knowing everything there is to know about an industry is understandable, particularly if you are just starting out, but you will need to have at least a general understanding of its composition, what functions it serves, and so forth. When connecting with industry experts and potential hiring managers, it will be to your advantage that you are able to speak intelligently about your reasons for pursuing your chosen career. Let people know you have done your homework and that choosing your career path was not simply based on where the dart happened to land on the board. The more familiar you are with your target industry, the more seriously prospective interviewees will take you.

Beyond gaining more familiarity with the Industry in general, identifying a comprehensive list of firms is important for a couple of reasons: 1.) the more firms you identify, the more jobs you can reference; and 2.) the more firms you identify, the more potential interviewees you can target. Your aim will be to identify as many firms as possible without regard to geographical location. Some firms will be local, while others have a national and international footprint. An important consideration to keep in mind is that the informational interview can be conducted via telephone, Skype, or in person. You are not bound by any geographical limitations. You can just as easily interview someone in your hometown as you can someone who resides 2500 miles away. Regardless of whether you interview someone who works in your town or someone who resides in another time zone, they all have their own professional networks from which you may benefit. If you live in New York and interview someone in Los Angeles, there is a good chance he or she may have connections with people in your geographic area who might be interested in your qualifications.

We live the digital age where social and professional networks are truly global. Regardless of your current residence, anyone anywhere can open a door for you. Remember, as you try to identify specific firms as well as the people you wish to interview, you are only limited by your own available time and willingness to expend the energy it takes to conduct a thorough search. You may end up with 50 or more firms in your industry, so it is incumbent upon you to identify how many firms you are capable of juggling at a given time. Be sure not to rule out niche or boutique firms. Many of these types of firms were started by a single or small group of entrepreneurs who can provide you with helpful career advice and guidance.

Targeting Specific Jobs of Interest

Once you have compiled a list of firms in your target industry,you will begin the process of identifying specific jobs of interest within the individual firms. Virtually every firm has a 'Careers' section where you can view available jobs and apply. At this stage, rather than actually applying to these jobs, your goal here is to gather information about the criteria and qualifications associated with your target career. Gathering this important information will help provide some context about your own overall qualifications, and will aid you in the development of the questions used in your informational interview (discussed in Chapter 5). As you explore the qualifications associated with your jobs of interest, jot down the qualifications most commonly sought among the positions. This not only help you in the development of your informational interview questions, but will also help you gain a better sense of how and where you might fit into a particular organization, industry, or chosen career path.

Chapter 7: First Interview

"Strive not to be a success, but rather be of value."- Albert Einstein

The First Interview: These days the first interview is almost always over the phone. This saves time and money and you would not believe how many stroll through the revolving door of the phone interview before one gets to round two. Once scheduled, you must take the time to prepare for the Phone Interview like you would an in person interview. Basic items are researching the Company (101 and I promised I would not teach you this), coming up with good questions (search Google for ideas and use the ones that actually provide you value), and knowing your background inside and out. Also, what is the job that you are applying for? That is what you NEED to focus on.

This is really important because I cannot tell you how many people would say they were, "looking for anything right now" or list 3 or 4 careers that they would be interested in. I am not your friend. I am here to make sure you want to stay in the seat I have to offer for more than a few months. You can only make me feel good about my odds of keeping you by being consistent in your interest for the job you are interviewing for. As an example let's use a Sales role as the job you are applying for. I am going to ask you what types of roles you are applying for. The answer should be along the lines of, "I am really focused on landing a Sales position because I am money motivated and want the work I put in to directly impact my earning potential." That is a textbook answer. You just made me really happy and confident in your desire to be in a role like this one.

Another question that people get hung up on is, "Are you actively looking for other jobs?" This question gets people to overthink and I am convinced people look at us as the jealous significant other who wants to make sure you are only thinking about us. That is wrong. We want you to be actively interviewing or searching because it shows us you are serious about your life and career. If you are laying around on the couch watching Orange is the New Black with your resume posted thinking it will do all of the dirty work, you are sadly mistaken. You are in charge of you career. Show your initiative by showing how you are actively applying to positions and following up.

The next question is always, "What type of roles are you applying to?" This is another way for us to see if you are really looking to be in sales, nursing, financial advising, or whatever the job may be. Make sure you answer the same job title as the one you are applying for. There are no application police to turn you if you in fact are looking at other types of roles. Another way of saying this is to tell you to lie if you have to (lie only when it is about an intention, NOT a fact). If you intend to try out marketing too and this interview is for sales? Lie to my face and say you are only interviewing for sales. If you have 3 misdemeanors on your record and I ask for your disclosure and can/will be doing a background check to make sure you were forthcoming, do yourself a favor and tell me about it. Facts are facts and can easily be proven/uncovered. Intentions are in your brain and you can tell me exactly what it is that I want to hear without me ever really knowing them.

To piggy back on that, the reason I want you to lie about your intentions of finding sales, marketing, or an advertising job is because I want you to get the job. It is of my opinion that your interest in those other fields realistically does not affect your ability to perform in sales. But for some reason, the hiring manager/HR wants to find people focused on that one path. So, in this instance please just lie to me so I can continue with the stuff that matters.

In discussing what motivates you, it is so important to make sure that you are answering with a long term mindset. Speak audaciously and confidently about what you want to accomplish and why. The more human and real that you can come across, the better I can relate to you. I want to give an example of this. When I was interviewing for the Corporate Recruiting job, I was asked what motivates me in life and how this job could help me accomplish that. I answered, "What motivates me in life is the fear of dying an average man who could not provide a good life for his family. I want to be someone that not only my family and friends are proud of, but the person staring back in the mirror every day is proud of. The only person who knows how much I really gave at the end of the day is me. I am my own worst critic, boss, and supervisor and will always make sure I am putting in 110%."

Another important aspect is to be ready to discuss your background, especially if there are any "red flags" as we call them. If you have any gaps of employment, inconsistent work history, or have had more than 3 jobs in 5 years, you better be ready to answer for it. This is time to be honest and open about what has gone on and why. My advice to you is to try your damn best to not get into this position.

Is there anything remarkable about you? If so what? Examples of this are simple things you do to be a better contributor to society. Do you volunteer, read, write, learn, perform, mountain climb, wake board, dance, or anything that might be interesting? If you do or have, work it into the interview. Make conversation with the person interviewing you and you will pass the all-important "barbeque test." What is that? It is the test of whether or not the interviewer could see themselves interacting with you at a barbeque. The reason for this is to see if you will fit inside of the Company culture. An example of how I handled this when I interviewed is very simple. Where are they from? Regardless of where it is a very easy way to relate is to talk about the sports teams there. Most people are avid sports fans and this works really well. Out of 5 interviews that is took me to land the Corporate Recruiting job, 4 of them went into a ten minute or longer discussion of Football, Golf, and Wrestling.

If you are not a sports fan find anything that you can to relate to the person during the interview and go for it. I was engaged at the time of that interview and the 1 out of 5 that I did not bring up sports was with a younger woman who was wearing a big shiny wedding ring that was clearly new. It radiated off of her and she kept that hand visible no matter what she did during the interview. I worked in my engagement and sure enough she was recently married. We talked about wedding planning, cliché wedding questions from relatives, Honeymoon, etc. for 10 minutes easily. The interview ran over and she clearly enjoyed speaking to me because I related our life experiences during the interview. Remember, we are all people trying to make a living. We are interviewing daily so when someone stands out and makes our job more fun for that hour, we remember them.

Chapter 8: Perspective

We will cover a wide range of commonly asked and most challenging interview questions; however, this book is not an exhaustive list. A recruiter may ask you questions you haven't anticipated (I used to throw a zinger in occasionally). A question may seem unrelated to the job for which you are applying. We'll look at the common thread that cuts through all of them: perspective.

Perspective, in this case a recruiter's point of view, is very crucial. Their point of view on answers to the questions they throw at you will significantly determine whether your answers are the "correct" ones.

While there are many perspectives from which interviews may be conducted by different people, all of them have one common viewpoint: how will the organization or company benefit from hiring you? They want to know if you'll add something positive to the organization. You should convey how the company will benefit from hiring you.

If you're applying for the position of sales manager, the company is looking for someone who will help it sell as much of its goods or services as possible. If you're asked a question like, "What's your greatest strength?" choose a strength that will best help the company's sales, not a skill that is unrelated. Having an "easy-going attitude" or good organizational skills may be less impactful than if you emphasize tenacity, perseverance, and/or getting people to trust you.

Even when asked to summarize your career, do so in a way that enables the recruiter to visualize you as an integral part of the team. When you think of how you'll summarize your career, consider how you can highlight your milestones best related to selling.

Remember, the interview isn't about you – it's about the company. Yes, they are interviewing you and are asking things about you, but they are doing so to see if you will be a great fit for the company.

Remember the interviewing organization's perspective when answering interview questions to maximize your chances of successfully acing the job interview.

In the remaining chapters, we'll be discussing the most commonly asked and challenging questions you're most likely to encounter in job interviews. These questions have been categorized accordingly, where each chapter contains questions for a certain category.

The Funnel System

It's helpful to have a format for answering questions. To ensure your job interviewers can see your main points as you provide your answers to certain questions, compose your answers in an organized manner that will allow the other person to follow your thought process and get your point. For this, I highly recommend the funnel system.

It's a very simple system. Just picture a funnel – wide at the top and very narrow at the bottom. It represents the order in which you'll tell your answer story to this question. Start the story with general or broad statements, and as you progress with your story answer, you're narrowing down the scope until you arrive at the main point. If you were interviewing for a financial consultant position and you were asked, "Give us an example of how you determine what type of financial product is appropriate for a client", a sample answer using the funnel system would be like this:

Beginning (Very Broad):During every client conversation, I follow a specific process to understand their individual needs. I have a map in my mind. As the client answers a question, I know which direction I might take the client… which road I may guide them down.

Middle (More Specific):If I ask a client about how involved they want to be in the day to day management of their portfolio and they sound like they are eager to learn and want to be involved, I know I need to move them down the path of a solution that will keep them involved. So, I'd take them down the road of involvement and continue to ask questions to clarify where our path may take us next.

End (Very Specific): Here's a specific example. Yesterday, I was speaking with Jane Emory. She was a new widow. Her husband had taken care of all the finances. She was nervous and sad, but she wanted to honor her husband's wishes and what he built in the portfolio. The more we talked and the more questions I asked, it became apparent she also really had her own ideas on where the money should go. She wanted to be involved. She wanted to be more involved than her husband had been in the past. This took us down the conversation to the degree of involvement and what that meant to her. She wanted to learn before she just let an advisor take it over. She was also worried about what was in the portfolio. She was a lot more environmentally conscious and cared less about making money and more about doing it in a way that was consistent with her values. After taking her through the process I have laid out in my mind, she decided she wanted to work with me, and she took my recommendations. It was a $3,000,000 close.

Using such an approach allows the interviewer to get the big picture first, which is crucial for understanding the main point that'll be presented at the end. Answering such questions in an organized manner, such as the funnel system, will help you communicate your answers and increase your chances of successfully leaving a positive impression. It also gives you the opportunity to show your process and provide a results-oriented example.

The funnel system is a format that works well with "tell me about a time" and "can you please give an example of ..." questions. One of the most common questions you will be asked during job interviews is the tell-us-about-a-time-when or example kinds of questions such as:

Can you tell us about a time when you faced a challenge...?

Can you tell us about a time when you had to choose...?

Can you tell us about a time when you were being forced to…?

Can you tell us about a time when you did something…?

Can you tell us about a time when you considered…?

Give us an example of how you measured success…

Give a specific example of how you executed against that strategy…

Give us an example of when coaching didn't work well….

While it may seem easy to answer these questions, it's another issue altogether how to answer them in a way that the interviewer will understand what you're trying to say. It's not unusual for job interviewees to think they explained their answers well, only to find they didn't when they failed to get the job. Start broad, so they understand your thinking… go narrow and get detailed, so they know it's a real example and you can demonstrate measured success.

Chapter 9: Tips For Preparing For The Interview

Dressing for Success in an Interview

Did you know that before you speak a word to the interviewer, you have made an impression by the way you dressed? Well, that is correct; most companies have different dress codes, and the way you dress for work may not be the same as your dress style for the interview. So, what is the best outfit you should put on when going for an interview? This will significantly vary based on the type of company as well as the job you are applying for. The guidelines provided here are generally accepted as appropriate for interviews, which will include advice on the things to wear, things you should not wear and how you can impress your prospective employer.

Business/professional Interview Attire

As I earlier mentioned, the first impression you make is usually the most crucial one. The interviewer will make his first judgment about you based on your appearance and on what you are wearing. You need to wear a business or professional attire. For men, this might be a suit jacket, slacks, and shirt with a tie, (a sweater is optional) and button down. For women, this might be a blouse and dress pants or a statement dress. It is also possible to add some modern style trends to your outfit. Also, consider the colors you want to wear for an interview; wearing clothes that are too bright or flashy might distract the hiring manager.

Business Casual Interview Attire

You can go for the non-professional attire if you are dressing for an informal work environment. The suit is more formal than business casual outfits. However, business casual outfits are more polished and professional than outfits like t-shirt and shorts or an outfit like a sundress and sandals. However, ensure you know the dress code before assuming that business casual is okay. In case you are unsure, you can call the office or contact the person that scheduled the interview for advice. It is important to dress a bit more professional than the workers are in the hiring company. For instance, if all the employees are wearing t-shirts and shorts, you might consider wearing Khakis and a polo shirt.

Attire for a Casual Interview

If for instance, you are applying to a start-up company, you might go for something relaxed but also presentable rather than putting on a black suit and dress shoes. You can wear relaxed-fit khakis, cute top and dark-wash jeans.

Take Care of Your hairstyle and Makeup

You have several hairstyle options to choose from when preparing for an interview. Some are funky while others are more traditional. However, whichever style you want, ensure that your hairstyle does not distract the interviewer. Ensure that your hair is polished and professional just like your entire outfit. What about makeup, especially for women? Well, it is also crucial that you make up correctly, but ensure that you do not make too much of an impression by applying excess makeup. Just like your hair, when you overdo your makeup, it could also distract the interviewer.

General Interview Attire Tips

Before the interview, ensure that you have the right interview attire and all things fit perfectly

In case your clothes are "dry clean only," then quickly take them to the cleaners after the interview so you'll be ready for the next interview

Endeavor to keep your clothes are in order the night before, so you don't have to waste time preparing on the day of the interview

Have your shoes properly polished

Before entering the building take some breath mints for fresh breath

Do you have tattoos? Consider covering them

Do you have many piercings? Consider leaving some rings behind (a good rule is earrings only)

Limit your jewelry

Keep your nails neatly manicured

Men should limit the amount of aftershave

Generally, avoid wearing an unprofessional outfit when preparing for an interview because it can distract the hiring manager from other amazing qualities you possess. Remember, image is everything so take good care of your image.

The Perfect Time to be at the Interview Venue

There are so many things to consider when preparing for a job interview: your attire, what to say, your body language, etc. One of the things you must also consider is when to turn up for the interview because it is a great indication of how you will behave when employed.

When you are late, you will paint the picture of being bad at timekeeping. In addition, when you arrive too early, then it might signify that you are over-eager. So, what is the perfect time to arrive for an interview? Well, the ideal time mainly depends on the job itself as well as the company's culture.

First, you need to check your invite to see if it says that there are paperwork to fill out or if you will have to report to a different manager or a reception. Therefore, if it is just a standard job interview, which has no additional procedures before the interview, then you can arrive between 10 and 15 minutes before the interview time. You will have sufficient time also to locate where you should be in the building and settle down. By getting there earlier, you will risk messing up the company's schedule – do not forget that you may not be the only interviewee the company invited on that day.

In addition, when you come too early, it indicates that you do not respect their time because they might have a good reason why they gave you the slot. You might cause them to come out and welcome you even before they finish whatever they were doing. One way to kill time in case you arrived early is to locate a nearby coffee shop.

What about Arriving Late?

If for any reason you anticipate arriving late, try to give the hiring manager a call as quickly as possible. Once you are truthful about it and your excuse is not lame, then they will understand. One way to avoid getting late is to carry out a trial of the commute at least a day before the interview day, so you can have a precise estimate of how long it will take to get there rather than rely on traffic reports.

What to Do While waiting for the Interview

Now that you arrived 10 or 15 minutes early, what will you be doing with this time? Most applicants do not really know much about what they should do, but experts suggest that it is the best time to look at the mirror, take deep breaths and also other things that will keep you focused and calm. The 10 or 15 minutes you have is an excellent opportunity to put yourself into the right frame of mind and focus your energy on who you will be meeting. You should focus on the things you need to remember, and questions to ask.

So stay calm and be friendly with the security guards, the receptionists and whoever greets you. Sometimes, they will be reporting to the interviewer about your behavior when you arrived.

What do you want to be remembered for when you leave the building? This is the right time to create certain things that will increase your likeability and memorability. Avoid rehearsing because you might make your conversation look unauthentic and scripted. While waiting to be called in for your interview, take care of your posture, sit in a power pose so you will appear confident and focused

Things to bring to an Interview

Now that you have a job interview, it is a proof that at least, the hiring company considers you qualified for the job. The interview is your opportunity to prove to the company that you are genuinely qualified for the position. You have to show them that you have what it takes to move the company forward. One of the things you must do to increase your chances of getting the job is to go with some essential items to the interview. So, what are the things you must take with you when going for an interview?

You need a Copy of your CV

You must bring a few copies of your resume to the interview if you want to impress the hiring manager. If you are going to face a panel of interviewers, then you appear organized if you supply them with a copy of your resume. Also, having a copy of your resume in front of you during the interview for your reference while discussing your skills is perfectly acceptable.

The Details of your References

Although most people often write - "reference available upon request", however, bringing a paper which contains the details of your references to the interview is better. It is a perfect way to display your organizational skills and indicate how serious you are about getting the job. Ensure that your references are not related to you, and they are reliable in terms of providing a detailed account of your capabilities and competencies. Make sure you have their contact details such as their email address, phone number and names. Do not forget to bring with you a reference letter also if you have one.

Have a Pen and Notepad

This may sound silly, but when you have a pen and paper, it also indicates that you are organized. It is a silent indication of the statement "I've thought ahead". In addition, you might need to write down questions that you want to ask the interviewer. In case the hiring manager tells you something, your ability to write it down implies that you take the position seriously. Finally, certain positions may require you to deal with difficult questions and making a note will help you answer such difficult questions.

You need a Folder/Briefcase

Take a folder or a briefcase because you will be carrying papers with you. Ensure you have organized all the things you need ahead, so you do not forget anything by accident.

Have the Directions and Contact information

The last thing you need when going for an interview is to get lost. It will increase your level of anxiety significantly, and you might get to the venue late, which could cost you the job. So, print out the directions and if possible, write down the contact information of the interviewer on the directions.

Your Portfolio of Work

Although this will be based on the position you are applying for, you will need to provide samples of your work. So, think of the medium of the position; for instance, going to a digital agency with a printed work is not the best thing to do. Instead, it will be better to provide links to your online portfolio. Endeavor to select your best samples to make a good impression. If necessary, you can add things like client testimonials, target achievement results, commendations and company awards.

Other extras include notes you were given before in the run-up to the interview, few grooming tools in case of bad weather and things to help freshen your breath.

Chapter 10: Why Is It Difficult To Land A Job Of Your Choice?

The world has grown nasty since the Renaissance. You can no longer find a person doing something he enjoys. The main point of any randomly picked job would be finishing it and not enjoying it. A person who has had ambitious dreams regarding working on something he has always been passionate about is highly likely to be disappointed.

So, what are the most common problems faced while looking for jobs?

Lower pay scale

You have a brilliant degree from a prestigious university and yet when you apply at offices, you face interviewers that offer you lesser pay scales than what you deserve. A prime factor of hunting jobs is to not just work on what you enjoy but also receive economic remuneration according to what you deserve.

Lack of skills

The most embarrassing situation for any officially qualified person is to sit an interview and being told that he/she is under qualified for this job he/she has applied for. Lack in skills is often cited as a reason by interviewers while rejecting job applications.

Conflict between interest and work

You may be passionate about a certain field of work and yet you land a job that is highly paying yet not within your interest range. This is a very common phenomenon in corporate circles. It is important that you fully enjoy what you do. But a tussle between interest and work often kills the buzz.

Bad work environment

Despite how lucrative the offer is, if a workplace has a bad surrounding that is in contradiction to work ethics and congenial environment, job seekers are often discouraged from even applying for jobs.

Technical flaws in applications

It is not sufficient to simply be passionate about work. Wrongly or insufficiently filled application forms often get rejected at the first glance. A lot of job applicants who deserve being employed are let down because of lack of attention to technicalities in their resumes and applications.

Bad interviews

A candidate may have the best of qualifications in the market. He/she may have passed out from the most reputed university out there but if the interview stage of the process goes wrong, everything goes in vain. The significance of the interview stage is very much and shouldn't be ignored at any cost.

Being rejected is a common economic phenomenon associated with the job circles around the globe.

The factors mentioned above are only a handful of some of the primary causes that end up disappointing those seeking a job. The next few chapters are going to enlighten you regarding how to avoid the mistakes that are generally committed by absent minded and less dedicated job hunters.

Chapter 11: Only One First Impression
***

I've been on both sides of the resume. I've had to compose attention-grabbing attributes about myself on a piece of paper and hope that my words synchronized with some employer's ideal candidate for the open position. I've also had the responsibility of shuffling through hundreds of resumes to find a few that fit my job description. The truth is that each employer is looking for key words within their stack of resumes that correspond to the position they are looking to fill. Unfortunately, many of the resumes get one glance and then are thrown into the recycling bin. You only get one quick chance to clearly and positively represent yourself as an amazing applicant.

I've seen all kinds of resumes that try to grab attention in obnoxiously obvious ways: printing on thick cardstock paper, colored paper, glossy paper and any other type of paper imaginable. I've received electronic resumes with highlighted sections and underlined attributes. I've even received a resume in an e-card before. Though it might have brought a fleeting smile to my face, all of those resumes were quickly discarded. I was looking for a serious candidate for the position I had to offer. The way the resume is presented is like a first interview. You want to show up looking professional and ready to work, not show up in a comical outfit that makes the employer question your sincerity.

The resume itself should be a simple, yet elegant document. It needs to show professionalism in presentation, while remaining straightforward in content. Too simplistic and lacking in detail will represent a candidate that might be too elementary for the position. Too much detail will leave nothing to the imagination and overwhelm the reviewer. You want to give just enough detail to make the employer want to pull you in for an interview and ask questions about the points listed on your resume.

Formatting the Resume—Learning to Let Go

Your resume should not be more than one page. Period. I know you are much more amazing than can be contained in one page, but learn to let go of unnecessary information. List only the most prevalent key points under each company in your employment history, consolidating your job responsibilities and achievements. You should list a maximum of four companies in your employment experience.

Though this might seem like a simple task, it is one of the things people struggle with most when compiling their resumes. Edit, edit, edit. It is acceptable to adjust the margins a bit and even adjust the font size, but cut out the excess. If you cannot decide what to cut out, have someone else take a look at your resume to advise what parts are excessive. With the help of others' eyes, you can separate the facts from the fluff.

As you learn to let go, you can also learn to add more important attributes when you gain additional skills. Be a continual learner by taking comprehension classes on the latest business software, become familiar with Microsoft Office and the updates that have been made to those programs commonly used in the professional environment. As you gain more knowledge, highlight it on your resume and let go of a different skill that might be more outdated.

Highlight Your Attributes – Use Your Words

Growing up, whenever I was mad or frustrated, my mom would tell me to 'use my words,' encouraging me to find a way to express myself that was more meaningful and complex than just letting her know that I was mad. She wanted to know how I felt and what was driving my anger, rather than hearing any meaningless curse words spill from my lips.

In the same way, your resume should use expressive words that accentuate your abilities. My best friend and computer homepage is www.thesaurus.com, where you can find many ways to say the same word. Some word choices reach further or sound more professional than others. The key is to select the words that contribute most to the highlighting of your attributes. The thesaurus can also prevent you from sounding too repetitive when listing the key responsibilities of your selected positions. Avoid being the "one-word-wonder" when showcasing the variety of skills and responsibilities you've acquired.

Under your additional skills section, list those attributes that best pertain to the job description. Include the different computer and software programs in which you are proficient, as well as any other special attributes that increase your value as a candidate. For general resume purposes, it is best to list all business related skills, but ideally you will contour your resume for each application. See that your resume parallels what the employer is asking for in an applicant. For example, if the position calls for marketing responsibilities, choose past positions you've held that reflect marketing assignments or similar business.

Do not lie on your resume. Too much exaggeration will hurt you later in the hiring process. Though it might make you look better on paper, lying won't get you past the first interview. Interviewers use your resume to create questions that delve further into your work history. If the interviewer finds that you have misrepresented yourself, there will be a negative view of you as a potential applicant. No employer is going to want to risk hiring anyone who is dishonest.

Your best plan of attack is to be completely honest about your work history and acquired skills. Lying on your resume is only wasting everyone's time. Instead of exaggerating, become an expert at wording your job responsibilities and experiences in a way that sounds more professional.

Examples:

Instead of – Filing Client Reports

Try – Organized Client Files and Reports

Instead of – Answered phones and emails

Try – Provided superb customer service by answering questions and inquiries via phone and email

Instead of – Cleaned the bar area

Try – Maintained an immaculate workspace

By using a more colorful and sophisticated vocabulary, you are using the art of telling the truth. The resume should be a work of art or a compellation of elegant words that best represent you.

You don't have to be fully chronological with your job history, but if you are missing a length of time between jobs, be prepared to answer why there is a gap in your work history. Life happens. When I was creating my resume, I had a few jobs that lasted for a year or less, but felt as though I gained important experience from those particular positions. Some of jobs ended due to the economical and budget cuts, and others ended because I found better opportunities. I decided to list them on my resume because I knew that I had made an impression at the companies I worked with even if it was in a short amount of time.

Employers are knowledgeable of the current economy. They are aware that it is difficult to hold down a job in this market and will not usually be judgmental of short employment gaps. Again, you might be asked to explain the gap, but do not be embarrassed to say you were looking for employment during that time. It is honorable to put yourself out there for employment, as well as being honest about your efforts.

Be certain if you list a past job on your resume that you have a positive relationship with that particular employer. It's amazing how many people share a network, and the employer is going to use all of their resources to find out more about you. If you left any company with a negative impression, do not list them on your resume.

While looking to hire for an assistant position, I met with a candidate that seemed desirable, but when I contacted one of the previous employers, I got a mediocre assessment of the person, highlighting a pedestrian work ethic when I was looking for someone who would go above and beyond all expectations. Had it not been for the inferior report from the past employer, the candidate might have had a better chance at the position. Any of your previous positions on your resume should come with an employer that would write a raving reference letter for your character and work ethic. Sometimes it's not possible to get raving reviews from every employer, but at least leave each position with a positive impression so no harsh words can be said to harm your chances at another position.

Occasionally, exceptions may occur. A personal risk I took on my own resume building process was to list a job position that I held for one month. In this case, I left the company amicably, but I'm sure the employer wouldn't have had much to say about my work ethic since they had no time to make an assessment. The reason I decided to display this position on my resume was to create a question for the employer to ask. I wanted to highlight that I left the company because it was not a fit for me. It was important for me to express my belief that a person has to fit the specific work environment, and if it is not a fit, it can be counterproductive to all parties. I don't suggesting taking risks on your resume unless you are confident that you can portray these risks in a confident way.

Formatting – Use Your Space

You want your resume to take up a full page. Even if you don't have much work history, create a document that is full of information. Again, this is your first impression for the potential employers. Leave them wanting to invite you for an interview. There are many types of resume formats to use. You can find multiple formats of resumes on the Internet, all of which are acceptable. Find a format that looks professional to you and use it as a guide to create your own resume. Take the format and make it your own, personalize and customize it to represent yourself.

For one of my resumes, I used a simple and clean format that allowed me to share my academic achievements as well as my work history, and special skills. The education section allowed me to showcase my prestigious study efforts, but also allowed for my page to be filled. During school, I worked side jobs as a coffee barista, math tutor, dance teacher and aerobics instructor, but once I entered the professional world, I wanted my resume to reflect the job positions that were most relevant to the positions for which I was applying. By choosing a template that allowed me to highlight education and specific skills, while listing the three most applicable positions, I was able to submit a competitive resume.

Tailor your resume to correlate with the job descriptions of any open positions. If the potential job wants someone with many managerial qualities and experience in customer service, make sure your job history touches on past positions that would demonstrate those traits.

Help and Revision

When you've finished writing your resume, at the very least make sure to hit the spell check button. It is imperative that your resume does not have any grammatical errors on it.

When I receive an abundance of resumes for a job opening, my first way of narrowing down candidates is by eliminating any applicant that has grammatical errors on the documents they submitted. Your resume is the most important document when you are looking for employment and if you submit it with errors, the employer will already assume that you are not detail oriented and are careless with communication—two characteristics that are detrimental to your application.

It is always a good idea to have another person look over your resume. You can use your school career center, a trusted teacher, or a professional acquaintance. It is just healthy for your ego to have a second pair of eyes look over your work for constructive revisions or opinions on how to improve and strengthen your resume. Often times, being human, we get so wrapped up in the pride of creating a masterpiece that we fail to see all the flaws.

Continuously revise and rewrite your resume as you gain more work experience, acquire more professional knowledge, or earn more achievements. Potential employers want to see your most recent qualifications and how you've continued to better yourself.

Chapter 12: Overall Preparation

Get Your Resume Updated and Targeted to the Job

The first thing we need to do is make sure we have a highly targeted and updated resume to take with us to the interview. If you haven't done this then stop right now and get your resume up to date and optimized.

Since this is not a book on resume design and creation I am not going to get into it. I suggest you read our book "Resume Hack" for details on how to create a powerful resume. But let it suffice at this point that every line on the resume should point to just one goal. That is making you appear as the most perfect applicant for the job. Everything should be as relevant and impressive as possible.

Even though you submitted your resume to the company at application, you are going to want to bring several copies with you just in case the person or people interviewing you do not have a copy in front of them. Stranger things have happened and if they ask you for a copy and you don't have one that will start you off on the wrong foot!

There is not one perfect number of resumes to bring with you but I have found that having six copies is almost always enough to get through an interview. You also want a copy for yourself to follow along with so you make sure you give the same resume (especially dates!) that is on the resume.

It is also perfectly fine to update your resume if you have had significant changes since you originally applied for the position. With some companies taking several months to go through applications it is possible that something important about you has changed since you last submitted a resume.

Prepare Well & Relax More

The one very powerful thing about preparation is the mental benefits it carries with it. The more we prepare for something the more confident we become with our knowledge and abilities. They more we practice and learn and become more informed the more confident we become in our ability to answer any question or handle anything that might come our way.

It's just like studying for a test or taking practice exams. If you study hard and know the material inside and out you are not likely to be nervous during the test. That is because you know that you are well prepared. After all, if you got over a 95 on 5 practice exams chances are that you will do just as well on this one!

It is insecurity that makes us nervous. If we only know parts of something then we will worry about what might happen if we are asked about something we don't know. This will make us act and appear nervous. Since part of the in-person interview involves watching the appearance and mannerisms of the applicants, preparing yourself well and being calm will help you a great deal.

Being able to relax will help you think better and respond more accurately. It will allows your voice to relax as well so there is little or no nervousness in it. It will also help you to answer questions easily and without endless rambling on because you are afraid you didn't say enough in your answer.

Take Notes & Keep Records

As you go through the preparation process, be aware that you will go through a ton of information. Information you might not feel is useful or worth much at the time but might be valuable later on. So when you apply for any job, make a few notes about the research you did at that time. This will give you a starting point on which to base even more research. There is no reason to do anything twice if you don't have to.

If, for some reason, you didn't do any research before you applied and you managed to get an interview out of a non-targeted or specific cover letter, then thank your lucky stars but do your research now!

Also keep track of when you sent the resumes out, who and where you sent them and any other notes that might help you out later. If there was a personal recommendation or contact you used, remind yourself of that as well. Keep a sheet or paper (or more if necessary) for every job. If you get a request for an interview, pull this paper and add to it as necessary.

Good Enough is Not Good Enough

I know a lot of people who go through life looking at something they had done or created and thinking that what they did was "good enough". Now sometimes "good enough" will be good enough but when competing for a job that is certainly not one of those situations.

Good enough might be good enough when you know everything about a situation or application and you know what is needed. But when you are competing for a job you have no idea who your competition is and what they bring to the table. They might be pulling out all the stops while you sit back with your "good enough" approach.

The reality is that your resume and interview performance has to be good enough to get the job. And that definition of "good enough" is nothing short of your very best. So if you think that good enough really is good enough then be prepared to go out on a lot of interviews and submit even more resumes until you find one job where your "good enough" actually is good enough.

Go Out on "Test" Interviews.

My last suggestions is one that takes the most time and effort but could at the same time provide invaluable experience and information for you regarding interview performance. It involves going out on practice interviews.

In a perfect world you would apply for several jobs before the really important ones come along. This way you can go on interviews and see first-hand what they are all about. While you can read about them and prepare yourself for them, nothing is better than doing well on an interview and getting really positive feedback.

Most of us know what our career goals and plans are and have a rough idea where we should be at one time or another. When we know these things we can make sure we are ready for opportunities when they arise. We can apply for jobs we don't think we are ready for just to get an interview and perfect our interview performance and skills.

We can get in front of real life interviewers and see how they work and how interviews are conducted. We can sit down afterwards and review our performance and answers and determine what we did well and what we should change later on. All of this we do with one ultimate goal: To make sure we are prepared as possible for when the largest and most important opportunities come along.

Do yourself a favor and put some serious time and effort into the preparation phase of the interview process. Prepared people do better and go further than those who don't bother to do the things that can sometimes make all the difference. You might not think this is worth the time and effort but trust me, it is.

Chapter 13: How You Can Make Sure That You Are Chosen For An Interview

Interviews can be tough, if you want to stand a chance of landing the job, you have to be well-versed on the industry and company, and command a deep understanding of the value you're bringing to the table for your potential new employer.

Based on my experience and research on both sides of the interview table, here are my 16 best interview tips to help you land your next dream job.

BEFORE THE INTERVIEW

1. Research the company.

Did you know that 47 percent of hiring managers have eliminated candidates after an interview because they had little to no knowledge of the company? Nearly half of professionals are going into interviews without having a well-formed understanding of the company and what they do. Take the time to do your homework on the company's website, blog, social channels and Wikipedia. Be sure to check out their competitors and make a mental list of what differentiates them.

2. Find out who you're interviewing with and research them too.

With 43 percent of hiring managers reporting that cultural fit is the single most influential factor in determining which candidate gets the job, how you come across in your interview is a big deal. Based on your research and email conversations ahead of time, be sure you have as clear an idea as possible of how well you're going to relate with the people you're interviewing with, and prepare accordingly.

3. Prepare creative, insightful questions and craft your personal story.

Sure, some of the standard questions like, "Where do you see the company in five years?" can be useful in some cases, but make sure that the act of asking them doesn't compromise your own credibility. Depending upon your potential role in the company, the person interviewing you likely doesn't want to hear you asking about what the day-to-day activities will be--they want to hire an expert in your field, so act like one. Be sure to refresh your memory on your most relevant recent experience and craft an engaging story that effectively communicates your employment journey. Focus on how your experience will benefit your potential new employer.

DURING THE INTERVIEW

Here's an insightful statistic: Over 33 percent of hiring managers say they know within the first 90 seconds of an interview whether they'll make a job offer to the candidate. That makes your interview prep even more important.

4. Dress for the job.

Should I wear a suit or play it more casual? The real answer is, it depends on the job you're interviewing for. If you're not dressed for the job you want, you're not doing yourself any favors. A whopping 70 percent of hiring managers say they've eliminated candidates after an interview because they were too fashionable or trendy. Don't be afraid to ask how you should dress ahead of your interview.

5. Bring two extra copies of your resume.

This sounds like a no-brainer, but I'm surprised at how many people show up to an interview without any copies of their résumé--leaving it to chance that the person they're meeting with was given a copy, or had the chance to research them beforehand. Plan for the need to have a résumé for every person you're meeting with and you'll never be caught off-guard.

6. Perfect your handshake.

Some 26 percent of hiring managers say they've eliminated candidates after an interview because their handshake was weak. Mastering the art of the perfect handshake is required homework before heading into an interview.

7. Turn your phone off and arrive five to 10 minutes early.

It may seem like overkill with all of the options we have for silencing ringers and putting your phone on vibrate without actually turning the device off, but there's another reason you need to turn your phone off before an interview: so you won't be tempted to check it. You're at an interview for one purpose, and one purpose only: to land your dream job. Don't allow any distractions to creep in.

Naturally, you don't want to arrive late for an interview. If you're running late, call ahead and be honest as to what's setting you back. Aim for showing up five to 10 minutes early, as anything earlier can really throw a wrench into a busy person's schedule if they feel that they need to accommodate your arrival.

8. Use confident posture.

Some 33 percent of hiring managers say they've eliminated candidates after an interview because of bad posture. As you're waiting in the lobby, standing, and walking around the office, is mindful of how your posture looks to the people around you. Are you slouching, or confidently arching your back? Take a launch stance while standing, and keep your back arched while sitting down for conversation.

9. Use the triple nod when listening.

Some 38 percent of hiring managers say they've eliminated candidates after an interview because of a lack of smiling and engagement during conversation. With employers consistently citing having a positive attitude as one of the most important factors in choosing to hire one candidate over another, showing that you're excited and engaged while listening to your interviewer will go a long way in showing off your stellar people skills.

10. Use hand gestures while speaking.

Within reason, utilizing a healthy amount of hand gestures to illustrate your points will significantly help reinforce your communication skills and show them your confidence in what you're saying.

11. Maintain eye contact.

Some 67 percent of hiring managers say they've eliminated candidates after an interview because they failed to make enough eye contact. This is a big one for me, too. I have a difficult time trusting someone who's constantly looking down or around the room instead of confidently communicating with me. According to many studies, people who have strong eye contact are perceived as being more persuasive, a necessary skill that every company places value on.

12. Get the email address of everyone you speak with.

If you're unsure about the company-wide email naming convention, then be sure to ask each person you interview with for the best email address to reach them at. This will come in handy after the interview.

13. Ask when to expect a decision and with whom to follow-up.

If you're interviewing with multiple people, be sure to ask the hiring manager (or last person you interview with) when you can expect to hear back on the next steps. There's nothing worse than leaving an interview feeling left in the dark about when the company is looking to make a final decision. If you're paying close attention, how they respond will also tell you a lot about how they felt the interview went.

14. If you want the job, say so!

Don't allow there to be any ambiguity about whether or not you actually want the job. If by the end of your interview, you're still feeling excited about the opportunity and want to move forward with the company, you need to say it! Never leave anything up to chance with the interview process.

AFTER THE INTERVIEW

15. Send a follow-up thank you email.

Before you go to bed on the date you had your interviews, be sure to send a brief, personalized thank you email to everyone you met with earlier in the day. Make sure to mention a small personal detail, mutual interest, or topic point you discussed with each person, and it'll solidify your great impression in their minds. Bonus points for sending a handwritten card, which has become a much-appreciated lost courtesy.

16. Follow-up if you don't hear back soon (one week).

If you don't hear back within four or five business days of your interview, it's completely acceptable to follow-up with either the person who's been your point of contact throughout the interview process or the hiring manager for the position.

Keep the follow-up very short and seek to provide value, rather than coming across as pushy or as trying to nudge them toward making a decision.

Also;

A. Make sure you have strong cover letters and email introductions. If you send your cover letter through the mail, make sure it's one page. Email messages should be kept to around 3-5 small-ish paragraphs. Your paragraphs need to be brief as to not take up too much time. Include contact information and the best time and way to speak with you.

B. List your cell phone, home phone and the email address you use the most and let HR managers know how to best contact you through your preferred method. If you are currently employed or in a situation where you cannot return calls, make sure to leave a call back number, or list sometimes where you are free to talk.

C. Proofread your cover letter and email message. Do this over and over until you are sure that everything is in place and you have mentioned the position, company name and included any applicable contact information. Following these tips will help you to create cover letters and emails that will stand out to HR Managers and recruiters looking for their next candidate.

Chapter 14: What To Do Before The Interview

Interviewing is one part of the employment process that is truly frowned upon by many, and indeed not favored by the average employment seeker. Interviews are the gateway to successfully satisfying the requirements and needs of potential employers, by affording candidates the opportunity to present themselves in both a personal and professional light. The ability to successfully showcase both personal and professional ethics and talents during the interview process, is a sure fire formula for landing the employment position that has captured your work interests in the first place.

Important Facts About the Pre-Interview Preparation

Many candidates fail to take into consideration the important first steps that are needed in their efforts to "ace their interview" with a recruiter or potential new employer. The perfect interview is truly the result of the "perfect pre-interview" regimen. There are a handful of effective and very important steps that should be incorporated into your overall interviewing process, that are sure to enhance your face-to-face interview at the time of its occurrence. The following are a few useful tips to engage, prior to attending your actual first-phase interview.

1. Do extensive research on the company you are applying to in an effort to show that you have a sincere interest in working within their industry, and for their company. This indicates to a recruiter, or a potential new employer that you are not simply going through the motions of interviewing to obtain a job, but rather that you have a genuine interest in the industry, their specific company, and the current position being offered. By researching the company and its history and background, you afford yourself the tools needed to engage in informative and constructive conversation with your

interviewer. When you are able to present statistics, historical data, and current events about the company, your interviewer will not only recognize your dedicated interest, but will be every bit eager to discuss these topics with you. Conversations that are direct company related play an important part in the impression you make and leave with your interviewer. These company communications many times serve to enlighten both the candidate and the interviewer on subject matters of interest to both.

2. The night before an interview, it is truly important to eat a healthy meal, limit any alcohol consumption, and certainly get a great night's sleep. Each of these elements plays an important part in your personal appearance, and presentation at the interview. If you have not slept well the night before, or did not allot enough hours of sleep, it is certain that more times than not, your interviewer will be able to recognize your lack of focus, or attention since your body and mind are not fully

rested to embrace the interviewing task at hand. A good personal appearance at your interview is every bit as important as your work, skills, and professional presence. If, perhaps you are not fully rested, and your interviewer is able to detect this, then indeed they are apt to make note that the candidate may potentially be less productive, and focused than required, since their interview presence reflected the same.

3. Practice your interview skills in a mirror prior to attending your actual interview. Many times candidates will find it useful in building their confidence when they take ample time to actually "practice" their responses to potential interview questions. More times than not, an interview is going to ask you to share a certain piece about yourself with them, or even an important event that has occurred in your life, and why it was so important. In addition, interviewers are sure to ask you what you feel your greatest strengths are, and ask you to talk a bit about your recognized weaknesses as well. Practicing

these very important,and high impact responses in the mirror will definitely offer some peace of mind and assurance when you are able to view your own expressions, and hear your own words during this important "practice" phase.

Recognizing the importance of pre-interview preparation is sure to afford the candidate an extra level of confidence during the interview process, and is sure to contribute some degree of accuracy and professionalism with some of the obvious important questions that will be asked. Make certain to do your homework on the company, give special attention to your physical health and presence the night before, and practice, practice, practice. Following this simple pre-interview agenda will surely give some credit to your overall presence, and can truly make a difference in your interview outcome.

Chapter 15: Practice Asking Questions

People who have been on several interviews have heard this line, "Do you have any questions for me?" It may not be the exact questions but something similar has been asked by an interviewer. Time after time, people end up not asking questions from the interviewer. Asking questions is good. It shows interest in the available position. It shows that you are actually considering how the job will be a good match for you. In this chapter, we will go over how to ask questions that will leave a positive impression.

A powerful question to test the truth of the interviewer about the actual job duties is asking, "What are some of the challenges the next hire will face in this position." You are want to know what are the problems what you will face in this employment role. This is a great way to test the honesty of the interviewer. No job position is 100% perfect. List to what the challenges so that you will be prepared for your first 90 days of employment. You might want to actually make a few notes in your notepad about the answer to this question.

"What are the qualities of a successful manager in this position?" You are asking the interviewer to let you know what people in the past did that made them succeed at this job. Success is remembered. The interviewer might be trying to figure out if you can do the same or do it even better. Their response will give an insight to what they will expect from you as a manager.

If you want to find out if the actual interviewer is hesitant about hiring you then ask, "Are you hesitant about hiring me due to my qualifications?" This question puts you in a very vulnerable position if you don't have thick skin. It also help put it all out on the table any concerns about your qualification. Be prepared to provide follow up information about turning your weakness into a strength in case the interviewer provides a reason that make them hesitant about hiring you.

"Where do you see the company (or department) in three years and how would I contribute to this vision?" This is a question to ask to let you know what are the company's or department's goals for the future. You want to know if they planning growth or is there no vision for the future as a company or department.

If you want to know whether you will need to look for another job as you are starting this job then ask about turnover. "What is your turnover rate for this department?" If there is no one else in with your job title or in your department then ask, "What's the turnover rate for the company?" Companies that retain employees are quick to answer with the amount of years people have worked at the company and interviewers who have been with the company more than a year have no problem voluntarily telling you have long they have worked at the company. Proceed with caution any time you have a department or company that do not have longevity with employees.

Here are a list of other questions to ask the interviewer:

What does a typical day look like?

How do you evaluate success here?

How would you describe the work environment here—is the work typically collaborative or more independent?

What types of skills is the team missing that you're looking to fill with the next hire?

Is this a new role that has been created?

What new skills can I hope to learn here?

If you could improve one thing about the company, what would it be?

What's different about working here than anywhere else you've worked?

What are the most important things you'd like to see someone accomplish in the first 30, 60, and 90 days on the job?

Who do you consider your major competitors? How are you better?

What do you like most about working for this company?

What are the next steps in the interview process?

After you have asked your questions, thank the interviewer for answering questions to help you better understand the position, team, and company.

Chapter 16: Preparing For The Interview

It is completely natural to feel nervous before a job interview but try to minimize pre-interview jitters with some preparation. You should do some research on the company you applied for before being called in for an interview. You will never know exactly what is going to be asked of you (unless you have an inside source), but you can do some through research.

-Look up the company website and study the history, about the products and services that are offered. Although you may not be quizzed on the origin of the company, it will give you insight into how the company operates and their philosophy. All of these factors should influence how you answer your questions.

-If you are applying for a sales position, you can be prepared for any role playing questions because you have taken the time to learn the company's products and services. It will be impressive to your interviewer that you have taken the time to research the information. It shows a commitment to details and a true interest in the company.

-Another way to prepare for an interview is to complete a practice run with a friend co-worker or family member. Have them ask you questions and answer them as if you were already in the interview, don't break character during the role play either. There are many questions that are asked in a typical interview (what are your strengths and weaknesses) don't let them come as a surprise to you – practice so you can answer with confidence.

Procedural Questions Asked In The Interview

Procedures are a part of life, especially in the working world. Each company has their own set of policies and procedures that they expect their employees to follow. An interviewer is going to ask questions to determine if you would follow protocol (for instance making a sale or handling a customer complaint).

Without specific training, you will not know with any degree of certainty how the company would want you to handle different situations but there are ways to answer that can increase your chances of getting the job. What an interviewer is looking for in an answer is your philosophy towards handling circumstances that occur in the company. Your natural instincts and personality is going to be reflected at some point no matter what you have been trained to do. Questions like, "How would you satisfy a customer if they wanted to return an item after the return policy has expired?" can be tricky to answer. The best way to answer them is to begin with saying, "Of course, if hired I would abide by the company's guidelines – but in this circumstance I would further…"

By stating your answer in this manner you are showing that you recognize a company is going to have its own designated policies and that you are flexible enough to modify your actions to align with those processes. Role playing scenarios are also used to test if your way of thinking is in line with the company's. This genre of question could backfire if your answer is completely opposite what the company is looking for. If you adequately researched the company prior to the interview you should have a good idea of how they handle customers and sales in general.

Bring Extra Copies To Interview

Always ask if there is anything specific you need to bring when booking the interview. Besides bringing your list of questions you should also bring duplicate copies of anything that you may need to provide to the interviewer in case there is more than one person conducting the interview. Even if you are not asked to bring references to the interview, take the time to type out and print copies anyway. Does not show up without any special documents that were specifically requested of you; if you do not think you can obtain them in the timeframe given be sure to let the person know before you arrive for the interview.

Never Be Late For The Interview

It is extremely important that you never be late for an interview. There is no excuse for it (besides an injury or family emergency). The interviewer doesn't want to hear about getting lost, bad traffic, or losing track of time. They are taking time away from their primary duties to sit down with you to try and give you a job so therefore it's rude and disrespectful to not show up on time.

Here are a few tips to ensure this doesn't happen:

-Perform a dry run: If you have an interview in a city or a part of the city that you are not familiar with then, do a test to gauge the driving time.

-Leave Early: Leave early enough to arrive into the area 30-60 minutes before your interview time. Don't go into the building but find a coffee shop and relax.

-Pay for parking: Don't circle the block looking for cheap parking on the street. Pay the money to park in a parking garage and elevate undue stress.

Consequently if you are running late make sure you call. The interviewer may have other plans and will not have time to complete the interview. Hopefully the interviewer will understand and be kind enough to book another appointment right away.

Chapter 17: Your Questions

Asking Questions

You will discover that there will be at least one time during the interview when you are asked if you have any questions, so be prepared for this. Mark down several questions that you would like to ask the interviewer. Don't ask just any questions, but questions that show that you have done your homework regarding the company. If you've done your research on the company, this shouldn't be too difficult. The important thing when creating your questions is to incorporate your research into the questions. Ask detailed questions that you'd only have knowledge about **IF** you have done your research. Here is an example.

Example:

Interviewer: Do you have any questions for me?

You: I know that {insert company name} has been a leader in the X product category for quite some time. In fact, they've held a dominant market share of over 40% for the past 5 years. Nevertheless, I know there has been some pressure by {competitor 1} and {competitor 2} recently. What steps do you see the company taking to hold on to their position and remain the leader?

Can you see how you start to combine pieces of your prior research? You are using the information you researched about the company and their competitors to ask an intelligent question that proves you've actually taken the time to do your research.

Questions to Ask

Besides showing that you've done research, you'll also want to ask questions for yourself. These types of questions allow you to get a feel for what the company is like and what you should expect. After all, both you and the interviewer are trying to determine whether you're a good fit, and that includes more than the operational aspects of this position. Let's take a look at two examples.

Examples:

What is the working environment of the company?

Every company is different, and you want to make sure that this company is a right fit for you. Some companies have a fun, relaxed atmosphere and some have more of a corporate, serious culture. Different people prefer different atmospheres, so this entirely depends on you. If the company is a huge Fortune 500 company, with a corporate culture, but you are looking to wear jeans every day, then this may not be an appropriate position for you.

What is a typical day like?

This question provides valuable insight on what to expect from the position. If you end up getting the job, this will be what you will be doing every single day. Of course, every job has its boring parts, but if the routine day sounds like something you'd hate, you'll be miserable. It's better to find this information out now, rather than later when it's too late.

It's important to reserve different questions for different interviewers. We will get into the types of people you will interview with later in the guide, but you should have some foresight into what person knows what. For example, a human resources interviewer may have a wealth of information about the culture of the company, but not specifics about the actual job function. These types of questions would be better suited for employees who are directly in the group you will be working with, such as the members of the group or a hiring manager.

Chapter 4.1: Mock Interviews

One of the best possible things that you can do before the interview process to prepare is to practice interviewing yourself. This will give you much-needed practice and help you feel confident prior to the interview. Do it several times, until you feel comfortable. Of course, it's not the real thing, but it's as close as you can get.

Write down your own questions and pretend that you are in the actual interview. Answer the questions how you would expect to answer them during the real interview. You should even dress how you would expect to dress during your interview. This will help you to take it seriously and make it feel authentic. You should record these mock interviews using a video or tape recorder and watch them after. Take notes on your interview and mark what you need to improve upon.

If at all possible, try to get a family member or friend to interview you. You can provide them with the interview questions and a sheet of paper, and ask them to mix it up (you should record this too). Afterward, ask them to give you their honest thoughts regarding what you did well and what needs improvement.

Chapter 18: Interview Techniques

Although we have discussed this topic briefly in earl paragraphs, it's a factor that all candidates must be aware of. As the interview board is supposed to view to the internality of candidates, they put different type of questions to you. They will not ask the same set of questions from all candidates because interviewers know that candidates discuss about the interviews among each other. We as members of interview panel always raise short questions to you and expect your answer in length. Idea is allow you to talk much while they listen to you. This is one of interview techniques, because when you talk in length all wanted and unwanted information will be released from your mouth. Immediately take notice of some points of your statement and note them down. This type of irrelevant statements will definitely stand unfavorable to you in the interview.

Anybody hoping to face interviews should take care of these hints and should not get caught to traps. Intelligent persons use their own interview techniques and escape. Interview techniques are applicable to both interviewers and interviewees. Sometimes they ask same question more than once. Candidate should be fully confident about what he/she talks. If you give two irreparable answers to the same question, there you are caught. It is advisable to answer exactly to the point and wait for the next question. Interview board uses interview techniques not to puzzle you but to get the truth out and to select the best person.

You have to be careful when they question you about your work experience and past employments. What you say in the interview should very well match with the information you have furnished in your bio – data (resume). What ever the interview techniques they try on you, you have to be firm, steady and in relaxed mood. When you get exited over questioning, you are definitely loosing some score. Determine every organization will go for persons with courage, enthusiasm and who can take up challenges. Everybody face interviews with intention of better their prospects. Somebody has to prepare you for the interview. In my opinion it's wise to conduct a rehearsal interview. Select few of your intimate friends, ask your friends to act as interview board and you may answer their questions.

When you do mistakes there is ample time for you to correct them. There should be at least one person who knows about interview procedures and the type of questions that should be asked. You have to do this rehearsal in the form of a case study, seriously do it, I am sure you will be motivated and developed to face an interview. Any wrong procedures, inappropriate answering has to be corrected then and there. This is something like practicing before a match. Good practices, determination with developed personality will always win challenges. It is of immense value to discuss important things with your Head of Department and other senior subordinates prior to interview. Being experienced persons they will guide you to the best of their knowledge.

Never be backward to exchange ideas with your colleagues because variation of ideas, expressions will carry you to the peak with their experiences, skills and job knowledge.

Telephone Interview

Some times they will like to interview you over phone. Mostly just after screening and short listing they decide to interview you over phone. In most occasions this will be a preliminary interview just to know some information. You may have to answer set of general questions. When they inform you in advance to interview you over the phone, discuss with the caller and set a time. Find a silent place for the telephone interview where you will not be disturbed. Now it's not a surprise because you were informed earlier. Mix your mood and attend to the telephone interview. I give below a set of specimen questions and answers as a guide line. Most probably in a preliminary interview they will not put you any tough questions. They will put you only some formal questions.

When you receive the interview call, you can wish the person, if the person does not introduce himself you can politely ask "may I please know to whom I speak now" Now we presume that interview is started. (Answer in a friendly & relaxed mood)

Q: Hello Shereen, What's your service in the present company? In what capacity you joined?

A: I am working there for six years now; I joined as an Accounts Executive.

Q: What made you to apply for this job?

A: I applied for a higher position to better my prospects.

Q: We really have a very tight work schedule, can you work under pressure?

A: Surely I can, I am used to that in my present place.

Q: Are you independent to work? Have you got any personal encumbrances?

A: I am very independent, no such encumbrances.

Well, thank you Shereen; we will get back to you soon. (Company representative ends the conversation) Now remember to thank the caller.

Email follow-up interview

Some company authorities do the preliminary interview by email. It is merely to save the time as they can't afford to spend time conversing over phones. Besides they think it is advantageous to send a questionnaire by a group email to number of persons at one time other than calling over the phone one by one. In case of a preliminary interview, I believe that this is a better system. You save time, telephone cost by using modern technology. Receivers of this email, have to reply back promptly. This system is little advanced than a phone interview because you can put some weight to the usually asked formal questions. Some company authorities convert this Email interview to a basic test paper, asking formal questions or put some technical sums to work.

You can do either way as a questionnaire or as a test paper with sums or to do some engineering formulas to test their knowledge. When the company receives the follow up email responses, they will short list only the persons whose answers are acceptable and correct. Questionnaire is prepared considering the job position. Candidates replying in a follow up email should take every effort to reply to the questions as per the company expectations.

If you are asked to brief a certain aspect of work, you should never write lengthy answers. If it is to be explained in detail, your reply should be appropriate to that. It is simple. In one way candidate has more chances in this to think and reply. In a phone interview or Skype interview your chances are limited as you have to provide answers on line. All candidates have to concern about "Attention to detail" when providing their answers.

On line Interview via Skype

Most of the company authorities universally use Skype to interview candidates as a source of modern technology. They select various methods of Skype interviews such as Skype video, Skype video using handsets and Skype chat interview. In case of Skype video Interview it is advisable to use your hand set as the conversation will be very clear. You have to adopt the same method. When they want to brief on some thing, please brief. When they want the answer in detail, you can write a description. Persons who keen on attention to detail will clear all these hurdles. When you do not understand their questions, your follow up reply will not help you to fare in the interview.

Proper coaching prior to interview and understanding the principals of the relevant employment sector will bring you marvelous results. Experience in the industry and practical job knowledge is the other factor that pushes you towards success.

I think now we have discussed about preliminary interviews in detail. If you memorize the contents we discussed it won't be a problem for you to get through the preliminary interview. When you get through preliminary interview, your next hurdle will be the first formal interview. This interview is conducted as a personal interview mostly. You have to dress smart; the costume should give a professional look. Do not wear just as you go to a special function. In this interview the interview board will see you for the first time and most probably the Head of the department, where vacancy exists also will be there in the interview board. Determine to give all of them a superb impression of you in the first interview, because first impression can take you even to winning post.

You must thorough about your general knowledge also. In this interview other than work related questions, they will test your general knowledge, whether you can work with people of different attitudes etc. They will check whether you are social in moving with multinational, multicultural generations. Look here some typical questions.
• General knowledge questions
• Your hobbies
• Family background

- Extra activities in school
- Sports activities
- Welfare activities
- Any other office bearing of societies in present work place

Chapter 19: Interview Etiquette

Before the Interview

You should ask at the time of setting up your interview who you will be interviewing with. Write down their names and memorize them! You might need to address them during the interview and if you can remember their names your attention to detail will prove to be a skill employers look for.

What to Bring

A bottle of water - It's common in an interview to be a little nervous and develop dry mouth while talking. If this happens just pause for a sip of water, and continue. Many places will offer you something to drink when you get there but you should bring your own small bottle **just in case** so you don't end up struggling to talk and swallow while you're trying to impress.

A Notepad and Pen – It's not necessary to take notes in an interview. Actually it's frowned upon because you need to be giving your complete attention to the interviewers and their questions. However, occasionally they may ask you to provide more information once the interview is over. You'll want to write down exactly what they want and who to send it to you, email address, fax number, etc. Write it down when they bring it up so you don't forget when the interview is over. You might not even need it, but again you should bring it **just in case**.

A copy of your Resume – They already have your resume. However, it's possible that they didn't make enough copies for the other interviewers in the room. Or worst case scenario, they simply misplaced it prior to the interview. You should bring a copy with you, **just in case**. Keep it in a folder so it doesn't get wrinkled.

A List of References – Checking references seems to be a dying trend these days because it's rare that employers get a candid response. However, some employers still swear by it so they might ask you for a list of references. These should be on a sheet of paper, separate from your resume. You should aim for three PROFESSIONAL references. Professional, as in someone that you've worked **for** or **with** in the past. Employers don't care about your personal references. Your friend from college or your neighbor offer zero insight into your work ethic and behavior on the job. I'll say it again, **your references need to be professional references**. If you've never had a job before, you can put down former teachers, coaches, or volunteer program leaders. **DO NOT** put down any family members.

Your list of references doesn't need to be elaborate. Just list the three people, first and last name, their title or profession, and a **working** phone number for them. For example:

John Smith, Assistant Manager at Cabelas - 555-555-5555

*You should always ask ahead of time if you can use them as a reference for job so they aren't caught off guard **just in case** someone calls asking about you.*

You might be noticing a theme here with all these **just in case** scenarios. Remember, preparation is the key to success so you should be prepared for every possible outcome.

What not to do

Don't make demands. There will be plenty of time to discuss what kind of salary you want and need, negotiate paid time off, or work out a flexible schedule to allow you to drop your kids off at school in the morning. Now is not that time. **Right now, your sole job is to sell yourself and make them want to hire you, not give them reasons to pass on you. IF** you can do that, you will be able to negotiate the details of an offer later on.

There are less formal interviews where some of these details do get brought up. If the interviewer wants to discuss it in an interview, by all means do so. Just remember, your job right now is to make them want to hire you so don't go making demands.

Don't look at your phone. It should be on silent or turned off. Better yet, leave it in the car. You will look pretty foolish if your alarm goes off or you get a call in the middle of the interview. Sounds like a no brainer, right? It's actually alarming how many people forget this simple gesture of respect.

Don't chew gum. It's annoying to hear your gum smacking or worse, to see it rolling around in your mouth while you're talking. Show some respect and spit it out before you get there. If you're worried about your breath chew a breath mint on the way to the interview.

Don't ramble on. The interview is a conversation between you and the interviewer(s). It's not meant to be dominated by either party. If you find yourself speaking for more than a couple minutes at a time, you might be talking too much.

For example, they interviewer might start by asking you to give them some information on your background (education, experience, etc.) and what led you to applying for this position. This is an open invitation to provide some good information about yourself. However, there isn't a lot of structure here. You can provide them with as little or as much detail as possible. DON'T RAMBLE ON. Keep it brief, **stick to the important highlights** and if they want more detail about something in particular, trust me they will ask. If you've had more than 10 years of work history, there's no need to go back further than that, unless they ask of course.

Confidence is Key

It's ok to be nervous. The interviewers are used to it and sometimes they are actually nervous too, especially if they don't do interviews very often. However, you **need** to be confident. **If they bring you in for an interview, it's because they already have interest in you and you have just as good of a chance at getting this job as the next person.** Probably more actually, since you're reading this guide to prepare yourself!

Sit up straight and make contact with whoever is speaking. Body language alone is a big indicator of confidence. It's also a big indicator of how you'll work on the job and interact with coworkers. You're telling them everything they need to know without saying anything. Easier than you thought, right?

If you get one of those more informal interviews where wages and salaries are discussed, definitely wait for them to ask you specifically what your expectations are. **My big tip for discussing wages and salaries when the time comes is to give them a range, not just one number.** It gives them some wiggle room and doesn't lock you into a number. For example, $15 to $18 per hour or $60,000 to $65,000 per year. Again, do your homework ahead of time on market rates for the position you are applying for so you can discuss this with confidence. Google search "market rates for [name of position] in [city, state]" or go to www.glassdoor.com and search there.

Chapter 20: Filling Out An Application

Filling out applications is sometimes easier said than done. Unlike certain things, not all apps are created equally. Some ask just the bare minimum and take a mere 15 minutes to fill out, depending on how much work experience or education you have, and others mimic the layout of standardized testing. A company I once worked for in Chicago, had an application that was over five pages long. I could see people getting arthritis, and others, carpal tunnel syndrome as they filled it out. It came complete with three essay questions and asked you to list your entire work history and also made sure to ask that you didn't put that apathetic phrase every hiring manager and recruiter hates to read, "Please see attached resume." All this was intentional, however. The company worked with an insane amount of paperwork and was in the sales industry. The application process was merely a foreshadowing of the true work to come, but also a good look and insight into the applicant's ability to be detail-oriented and write eloquently, or at least at a G.E.D. level. You can tell a lot about a person by the way they write. From their handwriting, to the words they choose, even their syntax tells you a lot about a person's personality and especially their level of education. You can tell how confident or shy they are by the way they write. You can tell if they're a neat and punctual person, crossing every "T" and dotting every "I," or a capricious and forgetful one.

The most important thing to remember when filling out an application is use current contact information. I can't tell you the number of people's phones that are disconnected when I'm following up on an app or resume I've received. Now, chances are, their phone is probably shut off because they're unemployed and are looking for a job, hence why I have their resume in the first place, but at least leave a phone number where you know recruiters and hiring managers can leave a message for you to call us back. You could get a Google number, I think those are free, or even use WhatsApp, also free. You could also list a close friend or family member's number instead of a number that's going to get disconnected in a few days if a payment's not made. Be smart and always make sure we can get a hold of you and that you can return our call, preferably before the end of the business day. Oh, and I can't end this chapter without saying DO NOT LIE ON YOUR APPLICATION. YOU WILL NOT GET THE JOB. Any information you put on your app is legally binding. So, protect yourself, and only put down information that is true and that can be proven.

Chapter 21: Proper Interview Scheduling

When you call to schedule an interview on your own, it is important to remember that there are likely to be others that also want to schedule interviews. Although it is more common for an employer to call applicants in which they are interested, some companies still publish advertisements in the newspaper and ask those who are interested to call to set up an interview. Although you may want to schedule something that is convenient for you, that may not meet with the schedule of the company. If you are interested in securing employment or new employment, you have to be willing to compromise.

When you call to schedule an interview, you have to be willing to take some time off from your current job, even when it is unpaid. Although this may not always be necessary, there are times you may have no other choice. For example, if the company is only interviewing this week, and there is only one slot left, you have to decide how important it is for you to secure an interview for that position. If you do not want your current employer to know you are looking for something else, you may have to think of an excuse or just state you have some personal business to which you must attend rather than lie about why you need the time off. In these cases, you are usually pretty informed about the time—if the schedule runs for an hour, you can be sure your interview will be within that period.

Choose times that are convenient for you and the company and ones that you will not have to change for anything other than an emergency. It is not good interview practice to schedule an interview at a time you are not sure of. Sometimes they will make allowances for some who might not show up—maybe because they felt that that person didn't appear to be really interested, so they will fit someone else in tentatively in case that should happen. They may also be unsure of how long an interview will take and will over schedule just to be sure that they can see enough people for the position.

Informal Interviews

Although it is not done much at higher position level, informal interviews are common in the executive areas. There is no reason this should not be a part of the interview process for other employees too. That doesn't mean engaging in a breakfast or lunch in order to discuss a new position. There are other informal settings in which one can engage in conversation about a new position. It tends to break the ice, especially for someone who may be coming in from out of town just to interview for the position. There is no law that says an interview must be conducted in an office or conference room, but most interviews do. It is definitely more professional.

One thing you must be careful of when having an interview outside and office is allowing the informal setting to distract you from the purpose of the meeting. Keep in mind that you are there to discuss a possible job and have simply chosen to do so informally rather than in the interviewer's office. This type of situation works well for those people who are against formal meetings or in cases where the interviewer may not want someone in the office to know they are looking for a new staff; maybe the new person is there to replace someone who is already there but failing to do a good job.

Relaxed interviews can be very helpful for those who have not had an interview in a long time or have just graduated and are a little nervous about looking for a job. It creates a friendlier atmosphere in which you can talk without being disturbed by visitors or by telephone calls. Make sure you stay focused on the interviewer and the topic discussed. Do not let your drink or food or other people around you distract you from being professional.

Interview Attitude: Failure vs Success

The way you carry yourself and the attitude you project to the interviewer have a great impact on your potential for being hired. There is certainly nothing wrong with attempting to sell yourself to the interviewer but you want to do it by drawing attention to your education and experience and not come across with an attitude that gives the impression you believe your skills are far superior to that of anyone else. Of course that is the image you want to portray—that you are the best person for the job—but you don't want to do it in such a way that it appears you are trying to convince yourself more than selling yourself to the company.

Another part that should remain concealed is that of your feelings about your current or previous employers. For example, if you were terminated because of something that was not your fault; do not make an issue of it by degrading the company or your supervisor. Most employers today will not give information other than your job title and the length of your employment; you can downplay the situation immensely. That does not mean you should lie about what happened, but do not go into much details—make it short, simple and nothing personal.

Under no circumstances should you enter your interviewer's office with any kind of attitude that is the result of something that happened before your interview—fight with your boyfriend, girlfriend or spouse, getting a ticket, or any other personal issues. When you arrive at your interview, you need to leave any personal issues outside the door so that you can present the best side of your personality to the interviewer. The interviewer could care less if you had a fight with your spouse before you left for your interview—all he or she wants is to find out if you are qualified for the position that is open with the company.

Some companies require a drug and alcohol testing; do not get irritated or offended by this. Your attitude and reaction will reveal a great deal to the interviewer, and if you appear agitated over the possibility of a drug test the message you will send is that you have something to hide and will most likely fail the test. That will cause the interviewer to skip over your application or chose someone else.

Chapter 22: The Interview: Facing The Panel The Right Way

For most job seekers, the most defining moment of the process is facing an interview panel. This is the time to either show your worth and crush the interview or let your competitors annihilate you. Most people experience an adrenaline rush during a job interview, which clearly manifests through restlessness, sweating, not responding to the right questions, and avoidance of eye contact. Before we delve into these, let's take a look at some sample questions that might be asked of someone seeking to be recruited. Practice answering the question for yourself based on the job you wish to apply for, taking special care to pay attention to the guidelines after every question. Also, in this sample live interview, we only take into consideration the questions that most employers, if not all, are likely to ask you –

you are in no way guaranteed to get all of these questions or only these questions.

Question One

Interviewer: Tell me about yourself.

Interviewee: (How are you supposed to respond?) However this may sound, this question does not want to know about your biographical data as captured in your resume or information relating to your age, where you come from, your religion, or your marital status. Rather, it seeks to find out your professional experience, achievements, and skills. In most interviews, this is will the first question asked, and unless you did some pre-planning and research, you will be disadvantaged and may not qualify for the position you seek to be recruited into.

Question Two

Interviewer: How much do you know about this company?

Interviewee: (Guideline for responding) This is another obvious but deceptively tricky question that companies or organizations will often post to interviewees early in the interview as a means of reducing the number of applicants successfully shortlisted for an interview to a more manageable number.

This question takes us back to Chapter One, where we delved into preparing for a job interview under the chapter heading: Information is Power. Companies today seek people who are reliably informed about the world around them, and this is a question that can make or break you during a job interview. To answer this question satisfactorily, doing prior research is important. This you can do by taking a look at the company's website and reading extensively about its services, products, management team, and structure, as well as other factors like its vision, goals, and objectives. Talking about the life history of the company won't win you a job.

Conclusion

Acing a job interview is all about staying calm, cool, collected and confident enough to deliver your message of interest in the company and fitness for the job. A lot of the confidence comes from being prepared to face the tough situation, which is what this little guide was intended for.

Now that you are armed with a lot of pointers, hopefully you can go out there and show the world what they are missing out on – you!

Take each interview seriously but not too seriously that your heart gets broken if you do not do as well as you hoped. Keep in mind that the most important thing you bring to an interview, to a job or to a company is yourself; so do not be too hard on yourself if you stumble sometimes. You'll get better at interviews the more of them that you experience.

www.ingramcontent.com/pod-product-compliance
Lightning Source LLC
Chambersburg PA
CBHW072014070526
44583CB00015B/1484